ROTOGRA

Specialist publishers of price guide reference books. Established 1959

Collectors' Coins - Decimal Issues of the United Kingdom

(formerly Check Your Change)

By Chris Henry Perkins.

4th Edition © 2017

ISBN (printed version): 978-0-948964-88-6
This title is available as an eBook edition and some of it's price data is also part of the Android™ app 'Check Your Change'.

A comprehensive UK decimal coin catalogue with values, descriptions and photographs

Special thanks to Sarah Grant, M McKerlie, Matthew Ahrens and others.

Errors and Omissions:

Every effort has been made to ensure that the information and price data contained within this book are accurate and complete. However, errors do sometimes have a habit of creeping in unnoticed, and with this in mind the following email address has been established for notifications of omissions and errors: info@rotographic.com. Readers within the UK can also call the telephone number below.

ROTOGRAPHIC

www.rotographic.com
020 308 69996

In Association with
predecimal.com

TABLE OF CONTENTS

INTRODUCTION

Welcome to the "Collectors' Coins - Decimal Issues of the UK" 2017 edition.

This inexpensive book, with listings and colour pictures of every circulated decimal coin type should provide an excellent guide to modern coinage and as such, should aid existing collectors and hopefully stimulate new ones.

Decimal coinage first appeared forty-nine years ago (the florin and shilling being replaced by the Ten Pence and Five Pence respectively, in 1968) and has become increasingly popular over the last few years. People want authoritative information without the urban myths, rumours and influence of media hype. This book has evolved over more than 50 years to provide that information.

NEW IN 2017

In late October 2016 it was revealed that the standard 2017 coins would be made available at the beginning of 2017, instead of at the end of the previous year, which has been the normal practice of the Royal Mint for many years and no doubt helped them cash-in on Christmas sales to people that either couldn't wait until the new year or bought them as gifts. No one knows why this has suddenly changed, but there is speculation that it may have something to do with the new £1 coin which will appear in circulation in March 2017. In January 2017 the annual proof set was released, containing the new pound coin, one commemorative 50p, two commemorative £2 coins and two commemorative £5 coins. I suspect there may be more commemorative releases during the year.

There was the odd impatient groan as people waited ages to see the 2015 coins in circulation. It wasn't until October 2016 that the last 2015 coin appeared in the wild - the 2015 Royal Navy coin (with 5th portrait of the Queen).

And there is a new £5 note, in case you hadn't noticed! AA01 prefix notes found their way onto eBay within what felt like hours of them being released and because everyone panicked that they would never see another of the almost 100,000 AA01 notes available it all went a bit silly (as usual). Prices seem stable now so I'll do my best to summarise in the £5 section towards the back.

The new £5 note and slow news periods seem to have encouraged the newspapers to run yet more stories on the valuable coins and notes you can find in your change. Unfortunately though, these stories are often either completely wrong or at best, only half accurate!

For example, recent tabloid revelations have informed us that the London 2012 Aquatics 50p with the lines on the swimmers face can sell for £3,000. This information was accompanied by a picture of the wrong coin in some reports. The truth is that the right coin (see page 42) usually sells for around £1,000. Just because some people may try to sell something for £3,000 doesn't mean they actually sell for that and factual information should always be based on verified actual sales. So, some element of truth - it is valuable - but on the whole quite mis-leading.

The same article also claimed that the 2011 Word Wildlife Fund 50p "commonly sells for £200-plus". I can only assume they missed out the decimal point and it should have read '£2.00' as on a good day, that's about as much as a normal coin from circulation will sell for (and in my opinion that's £1.50 too much!). Even the silver proof cased versions usually sell for £30 - £40. To tell people a normal coin is worth £200 is very mis-leading and frankly, bad journalism.

Anyway, back to this book - Lots of price updates and new information is contained within this edition as well as an expanded proof set section with a lot more price data for those, too. This edition is 16 pages larger than the previous and I'm afraid I've had to put the marked price up, for the first time in years, to £8.75.

I hope you find it useful.

Please do have a look at my new website, which is optimised for smart-phones and contains details of all the half penny to £5 coins made since 1968:
www.checkyourchange.co.uk
This book also has a Facebook group: Search there for 'Check Your Change'.
For news about the app to aid cataloguing your coins from circulation see p.68.

USING THIS CATALOGUE
The values listed in this catalogue are the result of many hours of compiling and comparing the prices offered by online dealers, online auctions, dealer sales lists, live-auction catalogues, and other sources. For some items, there is such a limited number of transactions on which to base the values that they may seem conservative.

Values are in the main, only given for coins in uncirculated condition. The reason for this is that with the high mintage figures of virtually all coins covered in this catalogue, any coin that is not in uncirculated grade usually has virtually no value above the face value. There are exceptions though and where certain coins in used condition have a current value above face value this is clearly shown in the listing under the 'Used' column.

MINTAGES

The numbers given as mintages are based on information available from many sources, including other reference works, online sources, and the Royal Mint. The accuracy of these numbers is by no means guaranteed, and modifications may be made as better information becomes available. It should also be noted that for some of the most recent issues, the mintages given are the "maximum mintages", and the actual number of pieces struck may be currently unknown. Again, updates will be made when new information is available.

COIN GRADES

The listings in this catalogue contain three prices, where applicable. The guidelines for these grades are as follows:

Used - A coin from circulation with normal wear and the usual bumps and scrapes from use. Most coins are just worth face value in used condition but for those that consistently sell for more than face value a 'Used' value is shown.

Uncirculated (UNC) - Appears as it did when it left the Mint. There will be no signs of wear or handling. May show "bag marks", as is common for mass-produced coins.

Brilliant uncirculated (BU) - A high end uncirculated. Fewer or no "bag marks" visible. At least 95%+ of the mint lustre should be present, but a lot of people will insist on full new lustre when buying BU coins. Most coins from Specimen folders or sealed packaging are considered BU. Brilliant Uncirculated is a term that the Royal Mint have used since the 1980s to describe coins they sell new in special packaging. Since then the term BU is also used for older coins and usually denotes any coin with no signs of use and full brilliant lustre.

Proof - A coin struck from specially prepared coin dies on a specially prepared metal blank. Because of this extra care, Proofs usually exhibit much sharper detail and have mirror-like blank flat areas (technically called the 'fields'). Some proof coins show frosted design details and such coins with contrasting raised design elements and mirror-like fields are sometimes called 'cameo', a term which originated in the USA.

THE VALUE OF GOLD

The price of gold influences the gold coin prices quoted in this book. The prices quoted here are based on a gold value of about £978 per ounce (£31,443 per kilogramme).

What's currently legal tender?
No half pennies are legal tender. They were demonetised on the 31st December 1984. Banks do accept them, but the high street financial institutions are not exactly falling over themselves to exchange the half-pee tiddlers!

Which are hard to find?
The 1972 coin was made as a proof only and went into sets, so is harder to find. The last coin, dated 1984 was also made for sets only.

OBVERSE

OBVERSE 1
(used 1971 - 1984)
D•G•REG•F•D•(date) || ELIZABETH II
Elizabeth II, Dei Gratia Regina, Fidei Defensor
(Elizabeth II, By the Grace of God Queen and Defender of the Faith)
Portrait by: Arnold Machin

REVERSES

REVERSE 1
(used 1971 - 1981)
Regal Crown
½ NEW PENNY
Design by: Christopher Ironside

REVERSE 2
(used 1982 - 1984)
Regal Crown
½ HALF PENNY
Design by: Christopher Ironside

INFO

Although it was known from the onset that the half-penny would see limited circulation, it was necessary to help facilitate the transition from 'old money' to decimal, as the old sixpence coins were still circulating as 2½ new pence.

TYPE 1 (obverse 1, reverse 1)

			UNC	BU	Proof
1971	1,394,188,250		£0.20	£0.50	£2.00
1972		Proof Only			£6.00
1973	365,680,000		£0.20	£1.00	£2.00
1974	365,448,000		£0.20	£1.00	£2.00
1975	197,600,000		£0.20	£1.00	£2.00
1976	412,172,000		£0.20	£1.00	£2.00
1977	86,368,000		£0.20	£1.00	£2.00
1978	59,532,000		£0.20	£1.00	£2.00
1979	219,132,000		£0.20	£1.00	£2.00
1980	202,788,000		£0.20	£1.00	£2.00
1981	46,748,000		£0.20	£1.00	£2.00

TYPE 2 (obverse 1, reverse 2)

			UNC	BU	Proof
1982	190,752,000		£0.20	£1.00	£2.00
1983	7,600,000		£0.50	£2.00	£2.00
1984	158,820	‡2	£2.00	£3.00	£5.00

NOTES

‡2   This year was not issued for circulation, and the "business strikes" were made for BU mint folders, only.

What's currently legal tender?

All 1p coins are legal tender. Merchants are allowed by law to refuse payments made in 1p or 2p coins if the combined total value of the 'coppers' is more than 20p in any one transaction.

Which are hard to find?

The 1972 coin was made as a proof only and went into sets, so is not likely to be found in circulation. In 1992 the Royal Mint changed from using bronze to using copper-plated steel. In that year both types exist and the bronze (non magnetic) 1992 coin is not usually found in circulation. Both bronze and copper-plated steel coins also exist for 1999, with the bronze coins distrubuted just within the year sets. See the end of this penny section for details on portcullis reverse varieties.

OBVERSES

OBVERSE 1
(used 1971 - 1984)
D•G•REG•F•D•(date) || ELIZABETH II
Elizabeth II, Dei Gratia Regina, Fidei Defensor
(Elizabeth II, By the Grace of God Queen and Defender of the Faith)
Portrait by: Arnold Machin

OBVERSE 2
(used 1985 - 1997)
ELIZABETH II || D•G•REG•F•D•(date)
Elizabeth II, Dei Gratia Regina, Fidei Defensor
(Elizabeth II, By the Grace of God Queen and Defender of the Faith)
Portrait by: Raphael Maklouf

OBVERSE 3
(used 1998 - 2008)
ELIZABETH•II•D•G || REG•F•D•(date)
Elizabeth II, Dei Gratia Regina, Fidei Defensor
(Elizabeth II, By the Grace of God Queen and Defender of the Faith)
Portrait by: Ian Rank-Broadley

OBVERSE 4 (similar to last, with no rim beading)
(used 2008 - 2015)
ELIZABETH•II•D•G || REG•F•D•(date)
Elizabeth II, Dei Gratia Regina, Fidei Defensor
(Elizabeth II, By the Grace of God Queen and Defender of the Faith)
Portrait by: Ian Rank-Broadley

OBVERSE 5
(used 2015 onwards)
ELIZABETH II•DEI•GRA•REG•FID•DEF•(date)
Elizabeth II, Dei Gratia Regina, Fidei Defensor
(Elizabeth II, By the Grace of God Queen and Defender of the Faith)
Portrait by: Jody Clark

REVERSES

REVERSE 1
(used 1971 - 1981)
Crowned portcullis
[OFFICIALLY: A portcullis with chains
royally crowned]
1 NEW PENNY
Design by: Christopher Ironside

REVERSE 2
(used 1982 - 2008)
Crowned portcullis
[OFFICIALLY: A portcullis with chains
royally crowned]
1 ONE PENNY
Design by: Christopher Ironside

REVERSE 3
(used 2008 to date)
Lower left section of the Royal coat of
Arms of the United Kingdom.
ONE PENNY
Design by: Matthew Dent

TYPE 1 (obverse 1, reverse 1)

		UNC	BU	Proof
1971	1,521,666,250	£0.10	£0.20	£2.00
1972	Proof Only (from the sets)	Used: £1.00		£6.00
1973	280,196,000	£0.20	£1.00	£4.00
1974	330,892,000	£0.20	£1.00	£3.00
1975	221,604,000	£0.20	£1.00	£3.00
1976	300,160,000	£0.20	£1.00	£3.00
1977	285,430,000	£0.20	£1.00	£3.00
1978	292,770,000	£0.20	£1.00	£3.00
1979	459,000,000	£0.20	£1.00	£3.00
1980	416,304,000	£0.20	£1.00	£3.00
1981	301,800,000	£0.20	£1.00	£3.00

TYPE 2 (obverse 1, reverse 2)

		UNC	BU	Proof
1982	100,292,000	£0.20	£1.00	£4.00
1983	243,002,000	£0.20	£1.00	£4.00
1984	154,759,625	£0.20	£2.00	£3.00

TYPE 3 (obverse 2, reverse 2)

			UNC	BU	Proof
1985	200,605,245		£0.20	£2.00	£3.00
1986	369,989,130		£0.20	£2.00	£3.00
1987	499,946,000		£0.20	£2.00	£3.00
1988	793,492,000		£0.20	£2.00	£3.00
1989	658,142,000		£0.20	£2.00	£3.00
1990	529,047,500		£0.20	£2.00	£3.00
1991	206,457,600		£0.20	£2.00	£3.00
1992	78,421 #1 Bronze		£3.00	£5.00	£5.00

TYPE 4 (obverse 2, reverse 2)
From now on, made of copper-plated steel (which is slightly magnetic)

1992	253,867,000	£0.10	£2.00	-
1993	602,590,000	£0.10	£2.00	£3.00
1994	843,834,000	£0.10	£2.00	£3.00
1995	303,314,000	£0.10	£2.00	£3.00
1996	723,840,060	£0.10	£2.00	£3.00
1997	396,874,000	£0.10	£2.00	£3.00

TYPE 5 (obverse 3, reverse 2)

1998	739,770,000		£0.10	£2.00	£3.00
1999	891,392,000	(#1 also in bronze)		£2.00	£3.00
2000	1,060,364,000		£0.10	£2.00	£3.00
2001	928,802,000		£0.10	£2.00	£3.00
2002	601,446,000		£0.10	£2.00	£3.00
2003	539,436,000		£0.10	£2.00	£3.00
2004	739,764,000		£0.10	£2.00	£3.00
2005	536,318,000		FV	£2.00	£3.00
2006	524,605,000		FV	£2.00	£3.00
2007	548,002,000		FV	£2.00	£3.00
2008	180,600,000		FV	£2.00	£3.00

TYPE 6 (obverse 4, reverse 3)

2008 #2	507,952,000	FV	£2.00	£3.00
2009	556,412,800	FV	£2.00	£3.00
2010	609,603,000	FV	£2.00	£3.00
2011	431,004,000	FV	£2.00	£3.00
2012	227,201,000	FV	£2.00	£3.00
2013	260,800,000	FV	£2.00	£4.00
2014	464,801,520	FV	£2.00	£6.00
2015	154,600,000	FV	£3.00	£6.00

TYPE 7 (obverse 5, reverse 3)

		UNC	BU	Proof
2015	418,201,016	FV	£2.00	£5.00
2016	Not yet known	FV	£2.00	£5.00
2017	Not yet known	Currently in sets only		

Special Sterling Silver Coins (Type 6 to 2015)

Sterling Silver pennies struck by the Royal Mint and available with pouches, marketed as gifts for new born babies.

			BU
1996	Unknown	Silver coin, originally part of a set	£20.00
2009	8,467	All below prices inc. original packaging	£15.00
2010	9,701		£18.00
2011			£20.00
2012	5,548		£20.00
2013	8,920	Plus 1,679 definitive silver pennies?	£20.00
2014		Royal Mint, price new	£30.00
2015		Royal Mint, price new	£30.00
2016	Type 7	Royal Mint, price new	£30.00

NOTES

‡1   In 1992, a change in alloy was made from bronze to copper-plated steel. In 1992 the original bronze planchets were only used for the BU Mint folders and Proof sets. The copper-plated steel planchets were used for circulation strikes only. The same thing happened in 1999 when bronze blanks were used in proof and BU sets.

‡2   The Dent reverse 2008 1p has been reported to exist with incorrect die alignment.

There are varieties of 1p coins that concern the rivets on the portcullis. It seems that for some years the coins in the BU sets (and proofs) were struck using different dies, resulting in two different types.

Both types of rivets (either circles as shown in the right image or dots as seen in the left image) occur for the following portcullis reverse coins:
1986, 1988, 1989, 1990, 1992, 1993, 2007, 2008.

What's currently legal tender?

All 2p coins are legal tender. Merchants are allowed by law to refuse payments made in 1p or 2p coins if the combined total value of the 'coppers' is more than 20p in any one transaction.

Which are hard to find?

The change from using bronze to using copper-plated steel has led to a couple of scarcer types. The 1992 coin made of bronze (i.e. non magnetic) is much scarcer than the 1992 coin made of copper-plated steel. Bronze and copper-plated steel were also used in 1998, although both types seem fairly common.

By far the rarest and most expensive 2p is the 1983 error coin, which has 'NEW PENCE' on the reverse, instead of 'TWO PENCE'. This mistake just affects the 1983 2p; no other coins have been noted with this error. The error coins went into sets and were not generally circulated. It is possible though, that some of the sets were broken up before the error was noticed, so there may be a few very rare 2p coins out there, in fact one turned up in change during January 2017!

OBVERSES

OBVERSE 1
(used 1971 - 1984)
D•G•REG•F•D•(date) || ELIZABETH II
Elizabeth II, Dei Gratia Regina, Fidei Defensor
(Elizabeth II, By the Grace of God Queen and Defender of the Faith)
Portrait by: Arnold Machin

OBVERSE 2
(used 1985 - 1997)
ELIZABETH II || D•G•REG•F•D•(date)
Elizabeth II, Dei Gratia Regina, Fidei Defensor
(Elizabeth II, By the Grace of God Queen and Defender of the Faith)
Portrait by: Raphael Maklouf

OBVERSE 3
(used 1998 - 2008)
ELIZABETH•II•D•G || REG•F•D•(date)
Elizabeth II, Dei Gratia Regina, Fidei Defensor
(Elizabeth II, By the Grace of God Queen and Defender of the Faith)
Portrait by: Ian Rank-Broadley

OBVERSE 4 (similar to last, with no rim beading)
(used 2008 - 2015)
ELIZABETH•II•D•G || REG•F•D•(date)
Elizabeth II, Dei Gratia Regina, Fidei Defensor
(Elizabeth II, By the Grace of God Queen and Defender of the Faith)
Portrait by: Ian Rank-Broadley

OBVERSES - continued

OBVERSE 5
(used 2015 onwards)
ELIZABETH II•DEI•GRA•REG•FID•DEF•(date)
Elizabeth II, Dei Gratia Regina, Fidei Defensor
(Elizabeth II, By the Grace of God Queen and Defender of the Faith)
Portrait by: Jody Clark

REVERSES

REVERSE 1
(used 1971 - 1981 and for the error 1983 coin)
Plumes in Coronet
[OFFICIALLY: The Badge of the Prince of Wales, with his
motto ICH DIEN]
2 NEW PENCE
Design by: Christopher Ironside

REVERSE 2
(used 1982 - 2008)
Plumes in Coronet
[OFFICIALLY: The Badge of the Prince of Wales, with his
motto ICH DIEN]
2 TWO PENCE
Design by: Christopher Ironside

REVERSE 3
(used 2008 to date)
Upper right section of the Royal coat of Arms of
the United Kingdom.
TWO PENCE
Design by: Matthew Dent

INFO

The current minting facility at Llantrisant,
Mid Glamorgan, was built in 1967 in order to meet
the demand for the millions of coins needed
for the conversion to the modern decimal
system now used in the United Kingdom.

TYPE 1 (obverse 1, reverse 1)

		UNC	BU	Proof
1971	1,454,856,250	£0.10	£0.30	£2.00
1972	Proof Only (from the sets) Used: £2			£10.00
1973	Proof Only (from the sets) Used: £2			£10.00
1974	Proof Only (from the sets) Used: £2			£10.00
1975	145,545,000	£0.30	£1.00	£2.00
1976	181,379,000	£0.30	£1.00	£3.00
1977	109,281,000	£0.30	£1.00	£2.00
1978	189,658,000	£0.30	£1.00	£2.00
1979	260,200,000	£0.30	£1.00	£2.00
1980	408,527,000	£0.30	£1.00	£2.00
1981	353,191,000	£0.30	£1.00	£3.00

TYPE 2 (obverse 1, reverse 2)

		UNC	BU	Proof
1982	205,000 [1]	£2.00	£5.00	£8.00
1983	631,000 [1]	£2.00	£5.00	£8.00
1983	Error, 'NEW PENCE' reverse Used: £200 - £400	£900.00		
1984	158,820 [1]	£2.00	£5.00	£6.00

TYPE 3 (obverse 2, reverse 2)

		UNC	BU	Proof
1985	107,113,000	£0.50	£2.00	£3.00
1986	168,967,500	£0.50	£2.00	£3.00
1987	218,100,750	£0.50	£2.00	£3.00
1988	419,889,000	£0.50	£2.00	£3.00
1989	359,226,000	£0.50	£2.00	£3.00
1990	204,499,700	£0.50	£2.00	£3.00
1991	86,625,000	£0.50	£2.00	£3.00
1992	78,421 [2] Bronze	£3.00	£5.00	£3.00

NOTES

[1] These years were not issued for circulation, and the "business strikes" were made for BU mint folders, only.

[2] In 1992, a change in alloy was made from bronze to copper-plated steel. The original bronze blanks were only used for the BU Mint folders and Proof sets. The copper-plated steel blanks were used for circulation strikes only.

[3] In 1998, both bronze and copper-plated steel blanks were used. It is estimated that about 55% of the mintage was bronze.

[4] In 1999, bronze blanks were used for Proof sets.

[5] A proof silver 1996 2p exists, it was originally available in a set.

TYPE 4 (obverse 2, reverse 2) From now on, made of copper-plated steel (slightly magnetic)

			UNC	BU	Proof
1992	102,247,000		£0.20	£2.00	-
1993	235,674,000		£0.20	£2.00	£2.00
1994	531,628,000		£0.20	£2.00	£3.00
1995	124,482,000		£0.20	£2.00	£3.00
1996	296,276,000 ‡5		£0.20	£2.00	£3.00
1997	496,116,000		£0.20	£2.00	£3.00

TYPE 5 (obverse 3, reverse 2)

			UNC	BU	Proof
1998	231,830,000 ‡3	Copper/Steel	£0.20	£2.00	£3.00
1998	About 55% of total ‡3	Bronze	£0.20	£2.00	
1999	353,816,000	Copper/Steel	£0.20	£2.00	£3.00
1999	‡4	Bronze Proof			£4.00
2000	583,643,000		£0.20	£2.00	£3.00
2001	551,886,000		£0.20	£2.00	£3.00
2002	168,556,000		£0.20	£2.00	£3.00
2003	260,225,000		£0.20	£2.00	£3.00
2004	356,396,000		£0.20	£2.00	£3.00
2005	280,396,000		£0.20	£2.00	£3.00
2006	170,637,000		£0.20	£2.00	£3.00
2007	254,500,000		£0.20	£2.00	£4.00
2008	10,600,000				

TYPE 6 (obverse 4, reverse 3)

			UNC	BU	Proof
2008	241,679,000		FV	£2.00	£4.00
2009	150,500,500		FV	£2.00	£3.00
2010	99,600,000		FV	£2.00	£3.00
2011	114,300,000		FV	£2.00	£3.00
2012	67,800,000		FV	£2.00	£4.00
2013	40,600,000		FV	£2.00	£5.00
2014	247,600,020		FV	£2.00	£5.00
2015	85,900,000		FV	£2.00	£5.00

TYPE 7 (obverse 5, reverse 3)

			UNC	BU	Proof
2015	139,200,000		FV	£3.00	£6.00
2016	Not yet known		FV	£3.00	£6.00
2017	Not yet known	Currently in sets only.			

What's currently legal tender?

Only the smaller post-1990 5p coins are legal tender. The older large coins can be paid into UK bank accounts at face value. The predecessor of the five pence, the shilling, should also be accepted at most UK banks as five pence. Check any shillings have no collectable worth using the Roto-graphic sister Publication "Collectors' Coins GB 1760 - 1970" before redeeming them at five pence face value.

Which are hard to find?

The old large 5p coins are no longer found in change (unless someone has managed to pass one off as a 10p, which sometimes happens). The scarcest are those that were made just to go into sets, or as proofs only: notably 1972 to 1974, 1976, a few of the early and mid 1980s coins, and the last large 5p struck in 1990. From 2012 onwards the 5p is made of nickel-plated steel and is magnetic.

OBVERSES

OBVERSE 1
(used 1968 - 1984)
D•G•REG•F•D•(date) || ELIZABETH II
Elizabeth II, Dei Gratia Regina, Fidei Defensor
(Elizabeth II, By the Grace of God Queen and Defender of the Faith)
Portrait by: Arnold Machin

OBVERSE 2
(used 1985 - 1990)
ELIZABETH II || D•G•REG•F•D•(date)
Elizabeth II, Dei Gratia Regina, Fidei Defensor
(Elizabeth II, By the Grace of God Queen and Defender of the Faith)
Portrait by: Raphael Maklouf

REVERSES

REVERSE 1
(used 1968 - 1981)
Crowned Thistle
[OFFICIALLY: The Badge of Scotland, a thistle royally crowned]
5 NEW PENCE
Design by: Christopher Ironside

REVERSE 2
(used 1982 - 1990)
Crowned Thistle
[OFFICIALLY: The Badge of Scotland, a thistle royally crowned]
5 FIVE PENCE
Design by: Christopher Ironside

TYPE 1 (obverse 1, reverse 1)

		UNC	BU	Proof
1968	98,868,250	£0.30	£1.00	
1969	120,270,000	£0.50	£2.00	
1970	225,948,525	£0.50	£2.00	
1971	81,783,475	£0.50	£2.00	£3.00
1972		Proof Only (from the sets)		£6.00
1973		Proof Only (from the sets)		£6.00
1974		Proof Only (from the sets)		£6.00
1975	141,539,000	£0.50	£2.00	£3.00
1976		Proof Only (from the sets)		£6.00
1977	24,308,000	£0.50	£2.00	£3.00
1978	61,094,000	£0.50	£2.00	£3.00
1979	155,456,000	£0.50	£2.00	£3.00
1980	220,566,000	£0.50	£2.00	£3.00
1981		Proof Only (from the sets)		£6.00

TYPE 2 (obverse 1, reverse 2)

1982	205,000 [‡]	£3.00	£6.00	£4.00
1983	631,000 [‡]	£3.00	£5.00	£6.00
1984	158,820 [‡]	£3.00	£4.00	£6.00

TYPE 3 (obverse 2, reverse 2)

1985	178,000 [‡]	£3.00	£5.00	£5.00
1986	167,000 [‡]	£3.00	£5.00	£4.00
1987	48,220,000	£1.00	£3.00	£2.00
1988	120,744,610	£1.00	£3.00	£2.00
1989	101,406,000	£1.00	£3.00	£2.00
1990	102,606 [‡]	£2.00	£4.00	£2.00

NOTES

[‡]   These years were not issued for circulation, and the "business strikes" were made for BU mint folders, only.

INFO

As of December 31st 1990, the large five-pence coins were demonetised.

17

OBVERSES

OBVERSE 3
(used 1990 - 1997)
ELIZABETH II | | D•G•REG•F•D•(date)
Elizabeth II, Dei Gratia Regina, Fidei Defensor
(Elizabeth II, By the Grace of God Queen and Defender of the Faith)
Portrait by: Raphael Maklouf

OBVERSE 4
(used 1998 - 2008)
ELIZABETH II•D•G | | REG•F•D•(date)
Elizabeth II, Dei Gratia Regina, Fidei Defensor
(Elizabeth II, By the Grace of God Queen and Defender of the Faith)
Portrait by: Ian Rank-Broadley

OBVERSE 5 (similar to last, with no rim beading)
(used 2008 - 2015)
ELIZABETH II•D•G | | REG•F•D•(date)
Elizabeth II, Dei Gratia Regina, Fidei Defensor
(Elizabeth II, By the Grace of God Queen and Defender of the Faith)
Portrait by: Ian Rank-Broadley

OBVERSE 6
(used 2015 onwards)
ELIZABETH II•DEI•GRA•REG•FID•DEF•(date)
Elizabeth II, Dei Gratia Regina, Fidei Defensor
(Elizabeth II, By the Grace of God Queen and Defender of the Faith)
Portrait by: Jody Clark

REVERSES

REVERSE 3
(used 1990 - 2008)
Crowned Thistle
[OFFICIALLY: The Badge of Scotland, a thistle royally crowned]
5 FIVE PENCE
Design by: Christopher Ironside

REVERSE 4
(used 2008 to date)
Middle part of the Royal coat of Arms of the United Kingdom.
FIVE PENCE
Design by: Matthew Dent

TYPE 4 - Reduced in size from 23.59mm to 18mm (obverse 3, reverse 3)

			UNC	BU	Proof
1990	1,634,976,005	Edge varieties	£1.00	£2.00	£2.00
		1990 silver proof pair, Type 3 and Type 4			£22.00
1991	724,979,000		£1.00	£3.00	£3.00
1992	453,173,500		£1.00	£3.00	£3.00
1993	56,945 ‡¹		£3.00	£6.00	£7.00
1994	93,602,000		£1.00	£3.00	£3.00
1995	183,384,000		£1.00	£3.00	£3.00
1996	302,902,000	(exists in silver)	£1.00	£3.00	£3.00
1997	236,596,000		£1.00	£3.00	£3.00

TYPE 5 (obverse 4, reverse 3)

			UNC	BU	Proof
1998	217,376,000	100,000 proofs	£1.00	£3.00	£3.00
1999	195,490,000		£1.00	£3.00	£3.00
2000	388,506,000		£1.00	£3.00	£3.00
2001	320,330,000		£1.00	£3.00	£3.00
2002	219,258,000		£1.00	£3.00	£3.00
2003	333,230,000		£1.00	£3.00	£3.00
2004	271,810,000		£1.00	£3.00	£3.00
2005	236,212,000		£1.00	£3.00	£3.00
2006	317,697,000		£1.00	£3.00	£3.00
2007	246,720,000		£1.00	£3.00	£3.00
2008	92,880,000		£1.00	£3.00	£3.00

TYPE 6 (obverse 5, reverse 4, Nickel plated steel from 2012 onwards)

		UNC	BU	Proof
2008	165,172,000 ‡²	£1.00	£4.00	£4.00
2009	132,960,300	£1.00	£4.00	£4.00
2010	396,245,500	£1.00	£4.00	£4.00
2011	50,400,000	£1.00	£4.00	£4.00
2012	339,802,350	£1.00	£4.00	£4.00
2013	378,800,750	£1.00	£4.00	£4.00
2014	885,004,520	£1.00	£4.00	£4.00
2015	163,000,000	£1.00	£4.00	£4.00

TYPE 7 (obverse 6, reverse 4)

		UNC	BU	Proof
2015	536,600,000	FV	£4.00	£4.00
2016	Not yet known	FV	£4.00	£4.00
2017	Not yet known	Currently in sets only.		

‡¹   1993 was not issued for circulation, and the "business strikes" were made for BU mint folders, only.

‡²   The Dent reverse 2008 5p has been reported to exist with incorrect die alignment of up to 180 degrees!

What's currently legal tender?

Only the smaller post-1992 10p coins are legal tender. The older large coins can be paid into UK bank accounts. The predecessor of the ten pence, the florin or two-shillings, should also be accepted at most UK banks. Check any florins have no collectable worth using the Rotographic sister publication "Collectors' Coins GB 1760 - 1970 " before redeeming them at ten pence face value.

Which are hard to find?

The rarest 10p is the 2009 coin with the wrong (previous) reverse! Only a couple of these are known so far. Perhaps there are more in circulation and it's certainly one that can easily be overlooked. The old large 10p coins are no longer found in change. The scarcest of those were made just to go into sets, or as proofs: notably 1972, 1978 and all of the large type coins from 1982 onwards. There are lots of known varieties for the Ten Pence, both larger size and current size. See the end of this section. From 2012 onwards the 10p is made of nickel-plated steel and is magnetic.

OBVERSES

OBVERSE 1
(used 1968 - 1984)
D•G•REG•F•D•(date) || ELIZABETH II
Elizabeth II, Dei Gratia Regina, Fidei Defensor
(Elizabeth II, By the Grace of God Queen and Defender of the Faith)
Portrait by: Arnold Machin

OBVERSE 2
(used 1985 - 1992)
ELIZABETH II || D•G•REG•F•D•(date)
Elizabeth II, Dei Gratia Regina, Fidei Defensor
(Elizabeth II, By the Grace of God Queen and Defender of the Faith)
Portrait by: Raphael Maklouf

REVERSES

REVERSE 1 (left)
(used 1968 - 1981)
Lion Passant Guardant
[Part of the crest of England, a lion passant guardant royally crowned]
10 NEW PENCE
Design by: Christopher Ironside

REVERSE 2 (right)
(used 1982 - 1992)
Lion Passant Guardant
[Part of the crest of England, a lion passant guardant royally crowned]
10 TEN PENCE
Design by: Christopher Ironside

TYPE 1 (obverse 1, reverse 1)

		UNC	BU	Proof
1968	336,143,250	£0.20	£0.50	
1969	314,008,000	£0.20	£0.50	
1970	133,571,000	£0.20	£1.00	
1971	63,205,000	£0.20	£1.00	£3.00
1972		Proof Only (from the sets)		£7.00
1973	152,174,000	£0.20	£1.00	£3.00
1974	92,741,000	£0.20	£1.00	£3.00
1975	181,559,000	£0.20	£1.00	£3.00
1976	228,220,000	£0.20	£1.00	£3.00
1977	59,323,000	£0.20	£1.00	£3.00
1978		Proof Only (from the sets)		£8.00
1979	115,457,000	£0.20	£1.00	£3.00
1980	88,650,000	£0.40	£1.00	£3.00
1981	3,487,000	£1.00	£4.00	£5.00

TYPE 2 (obverse 1, reverse 2)

		UNC	BU	Proof
1982	205,000 ⊞	£3.00	£4.00	£6.00
1983	631,000 ⊞	£3.00	£4.00	£6.00
1984	158,820 ⊞	£3.00	£4.00	£6.00

TYPE 3 (obverse 2, reverse 2)

		UNC	BU	Proof
1985	178,000 ⊞	£3.00	£4.00	£4.00
1986	167,000 ⊞	£3.00	£4.00	£4.00
1987	172,425 ⊞	£3.00	£4.00	£4.00
1988	134,067 ⊞	£3.00	£4.00	£4.00
1989	77,569 ⊞	£3.00	£5.00	£5.00
1990	102,606 ⊞	£3.00	£5.00	£5.00
1991	74,975 ⊞	£3.00	£5.00	£5.00
1992	78,421 ⊞	£3.00	£4.00	£4.00

NOTES

⊞ These years were not issued for circulation, and the "business strikes" were made for BU mint folders, only.

INFO

As of 30th June 1993, the large ten-pence coins were demonetised.

21

OBVERSES

OBVERSE 3
(used 1992 - 1997)
ELIZABETH II || D•G•REG•F•D•(date)
Elizabeth II, Dei Gratia Regina, Fidei Defensor
(Elizabeth II, By the Grace of God Queen and Defender of the Faith)
Portrait by: Raphael Maklouf

OBVERSE 4
(used 1998 - 2008)
ELIZABETH II•D•G || REG•F•D•(date)
Elizabeth II, Dei Gratia Regina, Fidei Defensor
(Elizabeth II, By the Grace of God Queen and Defender of the Faith)
Portrait by: Ian Rank-Broadley

OBVERSE 5 (similar to last, with no rim beading)
(used 2008 - 2015)
ELIZABETH II•D•G || REG•F•D•(date)
Elizabeth II, Dei Gratia Regina, Fidei Defensor
(Elizabeth II, By the Grace of God Queen and Defender of the Faith)
Portrait by: Ian Rank-Broadley

OBVERSE 6
(used 2015 onwards)
ELIZABETH II•DEI•GRA•REG•FID•DEF•(date)
Elizabeth II, Dei Gratia Regina, Fidei Defensor
(Elizabeth II, By the Grace of God Queen and Defender of the Faith)
Portrait by: Jody Clark

REVERSES

REVERSE 3
(used 1992 - 2008)
Lion Passant Guardant
[Part of the crest of England, a lion passant guardant royally crowned]
10 TEN PENCE
Design by: Christopher Ironside

REVERSE 4
(used 2008 to date)
Upper left section of the Royal coat of Arms of the
United Kingdom.
TEN PENCE
Design by: Matthew Dent

22

TYPE 4 - Reduced in size from 28.5mm to 24.5mm (obverse 3, reverse 3)

		UNC	BU	Proof
1992	1,413,455,170 [1]	£0.30	£3.00	£3.00
1993		£0.30	£6.00	£3.00
1994	56,945 In sets only	£2.00	£4.00	£8.00
1995	43,259,000	£0.30	£3.00	£3.00
1996	118,738,000 [2]	£0.30	£3.00	£3.00
1997	99,196,000	£0.30	£3.00	£3.00

TYPE 5 (obverse 4, reverse 3)

		UNC	BU	Proof
1998	In sets only (100,000 proofs)	£2.00	£7.00	£4.00
1999	In sets only	£2.00	£7.00	£4.00
2000	134,727,000	£0.30	£2.00	£3.00
2001	82,081,000	£0.30	£2.00	£3.00
2002	80,934,000	£0.30	£2.00	£3.00
2003	88,118,000	£0.30	£2.00	£3.00
2004	99,602,000	£0.30	£2.00	£3.00
2005	69,604,000 [1] '1' of '10' to bead or to space	£0.30	£2.00	£3.00
2006	118,803,000 [1]	£0.30	£2.00	£3.00
2007	72,720,000	£0.30	£2.00	£3.00
2008	9,720,000	£0.30	£2.00	£3.00

TYPE 6 (obverse 5, reverse 4. Nickel plated steel from 2012 onwards)

			UNC	BU	Proof
2008	71,447,000		£0.30	£3.00	£4.00
2009	84,360,000		£0.30	£3.00	£4.00
2009	1 or 2 known*	Mule rev. 3	£800.00		
2010	96,600,500		£0.30	£3.00	£3.00
2011	59,603,850		£0.30	£3.00	£3.00
2012	11,600,030		FV	£3.00	£5.00
2013	320,200,750		FV	£3.00	£5.00
2014	490,202,020		FV	£4.00	£5.00
2015	119,000,000		FV	£4.00	£5.00

TYPE 7 (obverse 6, reverse 4)

		UNC	BU	Proof
2015	91,900,000	FV	£4.00	£5.00
2016	Not yet known	FV	£4.00	£5.00
2017	Not yet known Currently in sets only.			

*	A mismatch of dies known as a mule has resulted in a couple (so far) of 2009 coins with the incorrect previous reverse (Ironside lion passant guardant).
[1]	Varieties exist for the 1992 issue, see next pages. Variety reverses 1 & 2 have also been noted for 2005 and possibly for 2006 dated coins. It is not yet clear if one type is scarcer than the other.
[2]	Exists as a silver proof, originally part of a set

TEN PENCE VARIETIES - Early, large size coins

There are a large number of subtle die varieties known for the Ten pence's struck from the earliest in 1968, right through to the 1980s. The varieties first came to light in the 1970s, surveyed (among others) by Ron Stafford, who published a few incredibly detailed articles on them. The majority of the varieties concern the number of beads in the borders and the precise positioning of the letters and digits, in relation to the border beads. It can make your eyes go funny just reading about it!

While significant, I feel that due to the complex nature, space required to list them all and the fact that the varieties are not often differentiated between, that it would perhaps be a better idea to mention them here, but not go in to any detail.

The original information on these early decimal varieties is hard to find, but there are however two highly recommended books on all 20th century coin varieties (including decimals) by David J. Groom entitled 'The Identification of British 20th Century Silver Coin Varieties' and 'The Identification of British 20th Century Bronze Coin Varieties'. Both are available new and can be found online.

TEN PENCE VARIETIES - Later, smaller coins

The production of the new 1992 smaller sized ten pence piece has yielded several varieties, some of which appear to be much less common than others.

The first type of ten pence pieces have a "wired" edge (left coin in both images), which has a curved edge, while all other varieties have a "flat" sharper edge (right coin in both images).

Obverse 1: The letters L and I in ELIZABETH point between 2 border beads. Obverse 2: The letters L and I in ELIZABETH point directly at border beads.

Reverse 1: The number 1 in the "10" points directly at a border bead. Reverse 2: The number 1 in the "10" points between 2 border beads.

TEN PENCE VARIETIES - Later, smaller coins

1992 Ten Pence types:

TYPE 1: wired edge, obverse 1, reverse 1
Earliest type. It appears that the "wired" edge was abandoned sometime midway through 1992 production. Represents approximately 40% of total mintage.

TYPE 2: flat edge, obverse variety 1, reverse variety 1
A continuation of the TYPE 1, but on different planchets with flat edges. This type also represents approximately 40% of the total mintage.

TYPE 3: flat edge, obverse variety 1, reverse variety 2
An extremely uncommon variety, referred to as the "between/between" type. Represents about 3% of the total mintage, perhaps a little less. This type could become desirable in the future.

TYPE 4: flat edge, obverse variety 2, reverse variety 1
The rarest variety, referred to as the "to dot/to dot" variety. Represents less than 1% of the total mintage, with some estimates as low as one half of 1%. This type may be worth saving for the future.

TYPE 5: flat edge, obverse variety 2, reverse variety 2
This type exhibits a new obverse and reverse style. Represents approximately 15% of the total mintage. This is the type is found in Proof sets and BU Mint folders.

From 1993 to 2006 it seems that the circulation coins all have Reverse 1 (i.e the '1' of '10' pointing directly at a border bead) and that proof coins and coins in the BU sets have Reverse 2 (the '1' of '10' pointing between two border beads). It is not known 100% if this trend continued up to 2008 (the last year of the old reverse design).

What's currently legal tender?

All 20p coins are legal tender. Victorian Double Florins also appear to be legal tender for 20p (4 shillings) as the author is unable to find any evidence that they were demonetised in 1971 with the rest of the old denominations. To spend one would be quite silly though, as the value of the silver contained within a double florin is far higher than 20p!

Which are hard to find?

The 1986 20p was made to be put in sets only and is therefore incredibly hard to find in change.

The new design 20p with no date is scarce. This coin is technically known as a mule and occurred because the Royal Mint used the old obverse (OBVERSE 3) with the new reverse (REVERSE 2) in error, resulting in a coin with no date on it. All the errors should have been dated 2008 as the Royal Mint noticed the error after about 100,000 of the first coins were struck.

The approximate mintage number of the mule 20p claimed by the Royal Mint of 100,000+ would seem to be supported by the quite large volume of these offered for sale. Clearly this is a very low number of coins compared to all of the other 20p annual mintages! But 100,000 cannot really be deemed as rare. 1000 would be scarce. 100 would be quite rare. It should be borne in mind though, that rarity alone doesn't always mean high values. High demand and not-enough-to-go-round is what causes things to be expensive. This is exactly what happened - all of a sudden thousands of people that wouldn't normally do anything with coins, apart from spend them, all wanted an error 20p and prices were very high after word got out.

Back to that low mintage number of about 100,000 - assuming that number is about right, it makes them approximately as scarce as the 1951 British penny. In the 1960s a similar thing happened (a little slower of course, because many people didn't even have televisions and the chap that invented the internet was still in short trousers) and the prices of known scarce coins were artificially inflated by people speculating that they would be a good idea to save for a rainy day. 60-odd years later and an absolutely perfect shimmering BU 1951 penny is worth less than £100 (in real terms, less than what people were paying for them in the 1960s). I could be wrong, but I suspect the same will be true of the mule 20p in 60 years time. They will remain collectable, but the demand will never again outstrip the supply and as a result the values will stay at a more realistic level.

I also predict that in the future the near perfect examples removed from circulation early on will be more sought after than the majority of the coins that were taken from circulation at the point of maximum hype after being used and abused for 6+ months. The 20p is a popular coin and many that I see for sale are far from perfect even after minimal circulation. Collectors can be fussy and some prefer the very best quality. The mule 20p has so far never been seen in any 2008 year sets.

OBVERSES

OBVERSE 1
(used 1982 - 1984)
ELIZABETH II | | D•G•REG•F•D
Elizabeth II, Dei Gratia Regina, Fidei Defensor
(Elizabeth II, By the Grace of God Queen and Defender of the Faith)
Portrait by: Arnold Machin

OBVERSES - continued

OBVERSE 2
**(used 1985 - 1997. Altered and made slightly
larger (right image) from 1992 onwards)**
ELIZABETH II | | D•G•REG•F•D
Elizabeth II, Dei Gratia Regina, Fidei Defensor
(Elizabeth II, By the Grace of God Queen and Defender of the Faith)
Portrait by: Raphael Maklouf

OBVERSE 3
(used 1998 - 2008)
ELIZABETH II | | D•G•REG•F•D
Elizabeth II, Dei Gratia Regina, Fidei Defensor
(Elizabeth II, By the Grace of God Queen and Defender of the Faith)
Portrait by: Ian Rank-Broadley

OBVERSE 4
(used 2008 - 2015)
ELIZABETH•II•D•G•REG•F•D•(date)
Elizabeth II, Dei Gratia Regina, Fidei Defensor
(Elizabeth II, By the Grace of God Queen and Defender of the Faith)
Portrait by: Ian Rank-Broadley

OBVERSE 5
(used 2015 onwards)
ELIZABETH II•DEI•GRA•REG•FID•DEF•(date)
Elizabeth II, Dei Gratia Regina, Fidei Defensor
(Elizabeth II, By the Grace of God Queen and Defender of the Faith)
Portrait by: Jody Clark

REVERSES

REVERSE 1
(used 1982 - 2008)
Crowned Tudor Rose
[The Badge of England, a royally crowned double rose]
20 TWENTY PENCE (date)
Design by: William Gardner

REVERSE 2
(used 2008 to date)
Lower right section of the Royal coat of Arms of the
United Kingdom.
TWENTY PENCE
Design by: Matthew Dent

21.40 mm • 5.00 grammes • cupro-nickel • plain edge

TYPE 1 (obverse 1, reverse 1)

		UNC	BU	Proof
1982	740,815,000	£0.30	£2.00	£4.00
	Silver piedfort proof			£20.00
1983	158,463,000	£0.50	£3.00	£4.00
1984	65,350,965	£0.50	£3.00	£4.00

TYPE 2 (obverse 2, reverse 1)

			UNC	BU	Proof
1985	74,273,699		£0.50	£3.00	£4.00
1986	167,000 ‡2		£4.00	£10.00	£10.00
1987	137,450,000		£0.50	£3.00	£4.00
1988	38,038,344		£0.50	£3.00	£4.00
1989	132,013,890		£0.50	£3.00	£4.00
1990	88,097,500		£0.50	£3.00	£4.00
1991	35,901,250		£0.50	£3.00	£4.00
1992	31,205,000 (both)	Small head*	£0.50	£3.00	£5.00
1992		Large head*	£1.00	£5.00	exists?
1993	123,123,750		£0.50	£3.00	£4.00
1994	67,131,250		£0.50	£3.00	£4.00
1995	102,005,000		£0.50	£3.00	£4.00
1996	83,163,750	*	£0.50	£3.00	£4.00
1997	89,518,750		£0.50	£3.00	£4.00

TYPE 3 (obverse 3, reverse 1)

		UNC	BU	Proof
1998	76,965,000	£0.50	£3.00	£4.00
1999	73,478,750	£0.50	£3.00	£4.00
2000	136,418,750	£0.50	£3.00	£4.00
2001	148,122,500	£0.50	£3.00	£4.00
2002	93,360,000	£0.50	£3.00	£4.00
2003	153,383,750	£0.50	£3.00	£4.00
2004	120,212,500	£0.50	£3.00	£4.00
2005	154,488,750	£0.50	£3.00	£4.00
2006	114,800,000	£0.50	£3.00	£4.00
2007	117,075,000	£0.50	£3.00	£4.00
2008	11,900,000	£0.50	£3.00	£5.00

* The 1992 small head coin was thought to be scarcer than the large head, but new information would seem to imply that the large head coins are the coins that were circulated in large numbers and are now hardest to find (especially in top condition as most have seen normal usage). It is now thought that the proof version only exists with the small head. The easiest way to tell the difference is that the small head bust has a much sharper point where the neck ends at the bottom.

1996 also exists as a silver proof, originally part of a set.

MULE ERROR (mismatching obverse 3 and reverse 2)

	UNC	BU	Proof
(2008) Also known as the 'dateless' 20p <u>Used, up to: £50</u>	£65	£85	-

Chinese made fakes exist. They have a dirty matt appearance, thinner lettering and a lack of detail.

TYPE 4 (obverse 4, reverse 2)

			UNC	BU	Proof
2008 [2][3]	115,022,000		FV	£4.00	£5.00
2009	121,625,300		FV	£4.00	£5.00
2010	112,875,500		FV	£4.00	£5.00
2011	191,625,000		FV	£4.00	£5.00
2012	69,650,030		FV	£4.00	£5.00
2013	66,325,000		FV	£4.00	£5.00
2014	173,775,000		FV	£4.00	£5.00
2015	63,175,000		FV	£4.00	£5.00

TYPE 4 (obverse 5 reverse 2)

			UNC	BU	Proof
2015	131,250,000		FV	£4.00	£5.00
2016	Not yet known		FV	£6.00	£6.00
2017	Not yet known	Currently in sets only.			

NOTES

[2]   Each year, it is determined, based upon supply and demand, what denominations will be struck for circulation. 1986 was not issued for circulation, and the "business strikes" were made for BU mint folders, only.

[3]   The 2008 new design (non mule) coin and also some 2009 coins exist with what was originally thought to be a small raised 'I' on the reverse. It is probably actually a die crack, rather than any deliberate mint identification. Interesting nonetheless, as a few of these are known to exist. This same 'I' die crack coin has also been reported dated 2010, but is yet to be confirmed.

2008 20p reverse with small 'I'.

Historically the Crown was five shillings (one quarter of a 20 shilling pound). Therefore the new decimal crowns initially had a face value of 25p. These four commemorative crown coins are legal tender for 25p, but they are rarely used by the public, probably because they are too big to be convenient, and to collectors they are usually worth a little more than face value. Members of the public often assume incorrectly that these four coins have a face value of £5, due to the fact that the crown was re-valued as £5 in 1990, although the size of the coin remained the same.

For later Crowns, see the FIVE POUNDS section.

These four coins were issued to mark the following occasions: 1972 – The 25th Wedding Anniversary of the Queen and Prince Philip. 1977 - The Silver Jubilee of the Queen. 1980 - The 80th Birthday of the Queen Mother. 1981 - The Royal Wedding of Charles and Diana.

COMMEMORATIVE TYPE I
Obverse: Standard portrait of QE II
Design by: Arnold Machin

Reverse: Elizabeth and Philip,
20 November 1947-1972
Design by: Arnold Machin

		UNC	BU	Proof
1972	7,452,100	£0.50	£1.50	£4.00
	100,000	.925 sterling silver proof		£20.00

COMMEMORATIVE TYPE 2
Obverse: Equestrian portrait of QE II
Design by: Arnold Machin

Reverse: Ampulla and anointing spoon, items used during the Coronation
Design by: Arnold Machin

		UNC	BU	Proof
1977	37,061,160	£0.50	£1.00	£4.00
	Specimen in folder		£1.00	
	377,000	.925 sterling silver proof		£15.00

COMMEMORATIVE TYPE 3
Obverse: Standard portrait of QE II
Design by: Arnold Machin

Reverse: Portrait of Queen Mother, surrounded by bows and lions
Design by: Richard Guyatt

1980	9,306,000	-	£1.00	£1.50	-
	Specimen in folder		£2.00	
	83,672	.925 sterling silver proof		£20.00

COMMEMORATIVE TYPE 4
Obverse: Standard portrait of QE II
Design by: Arnold Machin

Reverse: Conjoined busts of Charles & Diana
Design by: Philip Nathan

1981	26,773,600	-	£1.00	£1.50	-
	Specimen in folder		£2.00	
	218,000	.925 sterling silver proof		£20.00
Set of 4 (72, 77, 80 and 81) Crowns as silver proofs in large case. 5000 sets issued				£65.00

31

What's currently legal tender?

Only the smaller (post-1997) 50p coins are legal tender now. Most banks will allow you to pay in the pre-1997 larger 30mm coins.

Which are hard to find?

The most significant 50p that could possibly be found in change is the withdrawn Olympic Aquatics coin with the lines on the swimmers' face. See Commemorative Type 17. The prices for the Kew Gardens 2009 50p are also quite high, following media exposure when it was established a few years later that this particular coin has the lowest mintage of all the circulating 50p coins. The 1992-1993 EU coin is also higher priced after it was hyped up as being the old-size 50p with the lowest mintage.

In 2009 a complete set of coins featuring all the sixteen 1969 - 2009 designs was issued as cupro-nickel proof and sterling silver proof sets. All of them are the newer 27.3mm size and all feature the Ian Rank-Broadley portrait of the Queen (OBVERSE 4). See after commemorative type 5.

OBVERSES

OBVERSE 1
(used 1969 - 1972, 1974 - 1984)
D•G•REG•F•D•(date) || ELIZABETH II
Elizabeth II, Dei Gratia Regina, Fidei Defensor
(Elizabeth II, By the Grace of God Queen and Defender of the Faith)
Portrait by: Arnold Machin

OBVERSE 2
(used 1985 - 1997)
ELIZABETH II || D•G•REG•F•D•(date)
Elizabeth II, Dei Gratia Regina, Fidei Defensor
(Elizabeth II, By the Grace of God Queen and Defender of the Faith)
Portrait by: Raphael Maklouf

REVERSES

REVERSE 1 (left)
(used 1969 - 1972, 1974 - 1981)
Britannia
[The seated figure of Britannia]
50 NEW PENCE
Design by: Christopher Ironside

REVERSE 2 (right)
(used 1982 - 93, 1995 - 1997)
Britannia
[The seated figure of Britannia]
50 FIFTY PENCE
Design by: Christopher Ironside

DEFINITIVE TYPE 1 (obverse 1, reverse 1)

		UNC	BU	Proof
1969	188,400,000	£1.00	£2.00	
1970	19,461,500	£1.00	£4.00	
1971	Proof Only (from the sets)			£5.00
1972	Proof Only (from the sets)			£5.00
1974	Proof Only (from the sets)			£5.00
1975	Proof Only (from the sets)			£5.00
1976	43,746,500	£1.00	£3.00	£4.00
1977	49,536,000	£1.00	£3.00	£4.00
1978	72,005,500	£1.00	£3.00	£4.00
1979	58,680,000	£1.00	£3.00	£4.00
1980	89,086,000	£1.00	£3.00	£4.00
1981	74,002,000	£1.00	£3.00	£4.00

DEFINITIVE TYPE 2 (obverse 1, reverse 2)

		UNC	BU	Proof
1982	51,312,000	£1.00	£3.00	£4.00
1983	62,824,904	£1.00	£3.00	£4.00
1984	158,820 ⁺ˡ	£3.00	£8.00	£8.00

DEFINITIVE TYPE 3 (obverse 2, reverse 2)

		UNC	BU	Proof
1985	682,103	£3.00	£8.00	£8.00
1986	167,000 ⁺ˡ	£3.00	£8.00	£8.00
1987	172,425 ⁺ˡ	£3.00	£8.00	£8.00
1988	134,067 ⁺ˡ	£3.00	£8.00	£8.00
1989	77,569 ⁺ˡ	£3.00	£8.00	£8.00
1990	102,606 ⁺ˡ	£3.00	£8.00	£8.00
1991	74,975 ⁺ˡ	£3.00	£8.00	£8.00
1992	78,421 ⁺ˡ	£3.00	£8.00	£8.00
1993	56,945 ⁺ˡ	£3.00	£8.00	£8.00
1994	Smaller type. Marked 'ROYAL MINT TRIAL' Used: £1200.00*			
1995	105,647 ⁺ˡ	£3.00	£8.00	£8.00
1996	86,501 ⁺ˡ	£3.00	£8.00	£8.00
1997	⁺ˡ	£3.00	£8.00	£8.00

NOTES

⁺ˡ   These years were not issued for circulation, and the "business strikes" were made for BU mint folders, only.

*   Extremely rare 1994 'ROYAL MINT TRIAL' coins exist. The standard design is used. Round 1994 trial coins also exist. Not to be confused with commemorative type 3, which is also dated 1994!

OBVERSES

OBVERSE 3
(used 1997)
ELIZABETH II | | D•G•REG•F•D•(date)
Elizabeth II, Dei Gratia Regina, Fidei Defensor
(Elizabeth II, By the Grace of God Queen and Defender of the Faith)
Portrait by: Raphael Maklouf

OBVERSE 4
(used 1998 - 2008 and for most commemorative coins
1998 - 2015, except where shown)
ELIZABETH II | | D•G•REG•F•D•(date)
Elizabeth II, Dei Gratia Regina, Fidei Defensor
(Elizabeth II, By the Grace of God Queen and Defender of the Faith)
Portrait by: Ian Rank-Broadley

OBVERSE 5 (similar to last, with different alignment)
(used 2008 - 2015, with Reverse 4)
ELIZABETH II | | D•G•REG•F•D•(date)
Elizabeth II, Dei Gratia Regina, Fidei Defensor
(Elizabeth II, By the Grace of God Queen and Defender of the Faith)
Portrait by: Ian Rank-Broadley

OBVERSE 6
(used 2015 onwards, with variations for commemorative coins)
ELIZABETH II•DEI•GRA•REG•FID•DEF•(date)
Elizabeth II, Dei Gratia Regina, Fidei Defensor
(Elizabeth II, By the Grace of God Queen and Defender of the Faith)
Portrait by: Jody Clark

REVERSES

REVERSE 3
(used 1997 - 2008)
Often referred to as the 'Britannia issue' to distinguish it from the
commemorative issues.
[The seated figure of Britannia]
50 FIFTY PENCE
Design by: Christopher Ironside

REVERSE 4
(used 2008 to date)
Bottom section of the Royal coat of Arms of the
United Kingdom.
FIFTY PENCE
Design by: Matthew Dent

DEFINITIVE TYPE 4 - Reduced size from 30mm to 27.3mm (obverse 3, reverse 3)

			UNC	BU	Proof
1997	456,364,100		£2.00	£2.00	

DEFINITIVE TYPE 5 (obverse 4, reverse 3)

			UNC	BU	Proof
1998	64,306,500		£2.00	£5.00	
1999	24,905,000		£2.00	£5.00	£5.00
2000	27,915,500		£2.00	£5.00	£5.00
2001	84,998,500		£2.00	£5.00	£5.00
2002	23,907,500		£2.00	£5.00	£5.00
2003	23,583,000		£2.00	£5.00	£5.00
2004	35,315,500		£2.00	£6.00	£5.00
2005	30,354,500		£2.00	£6.00	£5.00
2006	24,567,000		£2.00	£6.00	£5.00
2007	11,200,000		£2.00	£6.00	£5.00
2008	3,500,000		£2.00	£6.00	£5.00

DEFINITIVE TYPE 6 (obverse 5, reverse 4)

			UNC	BU	Proof
2008	22,747,000		£2.00	£5.00	£3.00
2009	None for circulation*	(106,332 in sets) up to		£15.00	£10.00
2010	None for circulation*	(69,189 in sets) up to		£10.00	£15.00
2011	None for circulation*	(56,007 in sets) up to		£15.00	£15.00
2012	32,300,030		£2.00	£5.00	£5.00
2013	10,301,000		£2.00	£5.00	£5.00
2014	49,001,000		£2.00	£6.00	£6.00
2015	20,101,000		FV	£6.00	£6.00

* In used condition, probably a value of around £5 each for the 2009, 2010 and 2011 coins is
realistic. They are very rarely found in change.

DEFINITIVE TYPE 7 (obverse 6, reverse 4)

			UNC	BU	Proof
2015	Not known			£6.00	£6.00
2016	Not known	Currently in sets only		£6.00	£6.00
2017	Not known	Currently in sets only.			

COMMEMORATIVE TYPE 1
1973 || 50 || pence (centre)
Nine clasped hands forming a circle
(Britain's entry into the European
Economic Community)
Reverse design by: David Wynne
(also exists dated 2009, see page 37)

		UNC	BU	Proof
1973	89,775,000	£1.00	£2.00	£4.00
	Proof in leatherette case			£4.00
	Thick planchet but not recorded as Piedfort			?

COMMEMORATIVE TYPE 2
1992-1993 (upper) || 50 pence (lower)
Conference table with seats and stars
(completion of the EC single market and
the British Presidency)
Reverse design by: Mary Milner Dickens
(also exists dated 2009, see page 37)

		Used	UNC/BU	Proof
1992-1993	109,000	£20?*	£40/£50	£50.00
	Specimen in folder (including Britannia issue)		£60.00	
	26,890	.925 sterling silver proof		£50.00
	15,000	.925 sterling silver piedfort proof		£70.00
	1,864	.917 gold proof		£600.00

*Since being reported as the old size 50p with the lowest mintage, interest and prices have increased. Used examples aren't encountered that often.

COMMEMORATIVE TYPE 3
50 pence (lower right)
**Ships and planes taking part in the
D-Day landings**
(50th Anniversary of the D-Day Invasion)
Reverse design by: John Mills
(also exists dated 2009, see page 37)

		UNC	BU	Proof
1994	6,705,520	£3.00	£4.00	£4.00
	Specimen in folder		£5.00	
	40,500	.925 sterling silver proof		£24.00
	10,000	.925 sterling silver piedfort proof		£30.00
	1,877	.917 gold proof		£600.00

COMMEMORATIVE TYPE 4
1973 EU 1998 || 50 pence (lower)
Fireworks pattern of 12 stars
(25th Anniversary - UK entry into EEC)
Design by: John Mills
(also exists dated 2009, see below)

		UNC	BU	Proof
1998	5,043,000	£1.00	£4.00	£5.00
	Specimen in folder (including Britannia issue)		£7.00	
	8,854	.925 sterling silver proof		£30.00
	5,117	.925 sterling silver piedfort proof		£40.00
	1,177	.917 gold proof		£500.00

COMMEMORATIVE TYPE 5
FIFTIETH ANNIVERSARY (upper) || 50 pence (lower)
Caring Hands, holding sun's rays
(50th Anniversary - National Health Service)
Design by: Mary Milner Dickens
(also exists dated 2009, see below)

		UNC	BU	Proof
1998	5,001,000	£1.00	£4.00	£5.00
	Specimen in folder		£7.00	
	9,029	.925 sterling silver proof		£20.00
	5,117	.925 sterling silver piedfort proof		£30.00
	651	.917 gold proof		£500.00

The 2009 retrospective 40th Anniversary set of sixteen fifty pence coins.

From the introduction of the 50p in 1969 up to and including the 2009 Kew Gardens coin there were a total of 16 different 50p reverses used. These large types:

Standard Britannia with 'NEW PENCE' (REVERSE 1)
EEC Hands (commemorative TYPE 1)
Standard Britannia with 'FIFTY PENCE' (REVERSE 2)
EC 1992-1993 (commemorative TYPE 2)
D-Day (commemorative TYPE 3)

And also the smaller commemorative types 4 to 13 and the REVERSE 4 of the normal 50p.

All of these designs were sold in sets of 16, all featuring OBVERSE 4 and all being of the newer 27.3mm diameter, even the five listed above that were originally larger. Just over 1000 of each cupro-nickel or silver sets were made and they are both hard to find. Value: £380 - £450.

Very rare: There were also 70 gold proof sets and 40 gold proof piedfort sets sold!

COMMEMORATIVE TYPE 6
1850-2000 (upper) || PUBLIC LIBRARIES (lower)
Open book upon pillared building
(150th Anniversary - British Libraries)
Design by: Mary Milner Dickens
(also exists dated 2009, see page 37)

			UNC	BU	Proof
2000	11,263,000		£1.00	£4.00	£6.00
		Specimen in folder		£6.00	
		.925 sterling silver proof			£20.00
	5,721	.925 sterling silver piedfort proof			£30.00
	710	.917 gold proof			£550.00

COMMEMORATIVE TYPE 7
50 pence (left) || 1903-2003 (lower right)
Suffragette with WSPU banner
(100th Anniversary - Women's Social and Political Union)
Design by: Mary Milner Dickens
(also exists dated 2009, see page 37)

			Used	BU	Proof
2003	3,124,030	(43,513 proofs in sets)	£1.00	£4.00	£6.00
	9,582	Specimen in folder		£6.00	
	6,267 of 15k	.925 sterling silver proof			£20.00
	6,795 of 7.5k	.925 sterling silver piedfort proof			£30.00
	942 of 1000	.917 gold proof			£550.00

* Increased value recently due to someone 'discovering' 13 years later that 3.1m mintage is on the low side compared to most other 50p coins!

COMMEMORATIVE TYPE 8
50 pence (lower)
Runner's legs and stopwatch
(50th Anniversary - Roger Bannister's 4-minute mile run)
Design by: James Butler
(also exists dated 2009, see page 37)

			UNC	BU	Proof
2004	9,032,500	(35,020 proofs in sets)	£1.00	£4.00	£6.00
	10,371	Specimen in folder		£6.00	
	4,924 of 15k	.925 sterling silver proof			£20.00
	4,054 of 7.5k	.925 sterling silver piedfort proof			£30.00
	644 of 1,250	.917 gold proof			£550.00

COMMEMORATIVE TYPE 9
50 (upper) || JOHNSON'S DICTIONARY 1755 (lower)
Dictionary entries for Fifty and Pence
(250th Anniversary - Samuel Johnson's English Dictionary)
Design by: Tom Phillips
(also exists dated 2009, see page 37)

			UNC	BU	Proof
2005	17,649,000	[40,563 proofs in sets] £1.00	£1.00	£4.00	£6.00
	4,029 of 7,500	.925 sterling silver proof			£20.00
	3,808 of 5,000	.925 sterling silver piedfort proof			£30.00
	1,000	.917 gold proof			£550.00

COMMEMORATIVE TYPE 10
FIFTY PENCE (lower)
Representation of the heroic acts performed by VC recipients
(150th Anniversary - Institution of the Victoria Cross)
Design by: Clive Duncan
(also exists dated 2009, see page 37)

			UNC	BU	Proof
2006	10,000,500*	[37,689 proofs in sets] £1.00	£1.00	£4.00	£6.00
	31,266	Specimen in folder		£6.00	
	6,872 of 7,500	.925 sterling silver proof			£20.00
	3,415 of 5,000	.925 sterling silver piedfort proof			£40.00
	804 of 1000	.917 gold proof			£550.00

COMMEMORATIVE TYPE 11
VC || FIFTY PENCE
The obverse and reverse of the Victoria Cross
(150th Anniversary - Institution of the Victoria Cross)
Design by: Claire Aldridge
(also exists dated 2009, see page 37)

			UNC	BU	Proof
2006	12,087,000*	[37,689 proofs in sets] £1.00	£1.00	£4.00	£6.00
	37,176	Specimen in folder		£6.00	
	6,310 of 7,500	.925 sterling silver proof			£20.00
	3,532 of 5,000	.925 sterling silver piedfort proof			£30.00
	866 of 1000	.917 gold proof			£550.00

* Pair of Type 10 and Type 11 coins in folder: £15.00

| 27.3 mm • 8.0 grammes • cupro-nickel • plain edge |

COMMEMORATIVE TYPE 12
FIFTY PENCE | 1907 | BE PREPARED | 2007
The scouting badge
(100th Anniversary - The Scout Movement)
Design by: Kerry Jones
(also exists dated 2009, see page 37)

			UNC	BU	Proof
2007	7,710,750	(38,215 proofs in sets)	£1.00	£4.00	£6.00
	46,632 of 100k	Specimen in folder		£6.00	
	10,895 of 12,500	.925 sterling silver proof			£22.00
	1,555 of 5,000	.925 sterling silver piedfort proof			£40.00
	1,250	.917 gold proof			£550.00

COMMEMORATIVE TYPE 13
1759 2009 | KEW
Chinese Pagoda
(250th Anniversary - Kew Gardens)
Design by: Christopher Le Brun

			Used	UNC/BU	Proof
2009	210,000	(34,438 proofs in sets)	£65.00	£80/£110	£100.00
	128,364	Specimen in folder		£170.00	
	7,575	.925 sterling silver proof			£120.00
	2,967	.925 sterling silver piedfort proof			£200.00
	629 of 1,000	.917 gold proof			£1000.00

Prices for the Kew Gardens 50p are high due to an article in the Daily Mail online on the 20th February 2014 following a Royal Mint press release. Similar information was repeated by the Guardian and also featured the following day on BBC Radio 2. The article implied that they are somehow special. This caused people to pay way over the odds on eBay, which in turn meant that sellers started pricing them higher and it all got a bit out of control. The normal non proof BU coins were selling for £180 at one stage (and nearly £300 for the specimen in folder). Just a couple of days later the normal circulation coins were down to between £35 and £50. This was a repeat of the kind of media exposure surrounding the dateless (2008) 20p mule error which caused that particular coin to sell for hundreds of pounds before dropping back to a more realistic level (which, for most of the battered and abused coins that are sold is still too high in my opinion). The fact that people are aware of it, will probably have a residual effect on values.

A mintage of 210,000 (it's actually 444,696 if the single packaged coins and those in the BU year-sets are included) is very low compared the other fifty-pences that are currently in circulation, but there are plenty to go round, as there simply aren't anywhere near 444k people in the world that really want one to keep, not just to turn a profit on. Prices do fluctuate, increasing sometimes during slow news periods when some of the papers and tabloid websites re-publish the same old coin stories.

COMMEMORATIVE TYPE 14
50 PENCE
An Olympic High Jumper - Obverse dated 2009
(The young viewers of Blue Peter were invited to submit entries for the design - This was the winner)
Design by: Florence Jackson (aged 8)
Obverse: 4

BU

2009   Initially 100k were planned, it appears to have been reduced to a max. limit of 50k. Only 19,751 were sold.

Specimen on card only (this coin was not circulated)   £75.00

The mintage number of this coin wasn't made available until recently. Gradually people are realising that very few were sold and even though they were just a few pounds a few years ago, more people want one now and the increased demand has driven the value up.

COMMEMORATIVE TYPE 15
CELEBRATING ONE HUNDRED YEARS OF GIRLGUIDING UK| 50 | PENCE
Girl Guide emblems
(100th Anniversary - The Girl Guides)
Design by: Jonathan Evans and Donna Hainan

			UNC	BU	Proof
2010	7,410,090		FV	£4.00	
		Specimen in folder		£7.00	
	5,271	.925 sterling silver proof			£30.00
	2,879	.925 sterling silver piedfort proof			£55.00
	355	.917 gold proof			£575.00

COMMEMORATIVE TYPE 16
WWF / 2011
Animal and plant shapes
(50th Anniversary - Word Wildlife Fund)
Design by: Matthew Dent

			Used	BU	Proof
2011	3,400,000		£1 - £2	£10.00	£10.00
		Specimen in folder		£17.00	
	24,870	.925 sterling silver proof			£30.00
	2,244	.925 sterling silver piedfort proof			£60.00
	243 of 1,000	.917 gold proof			£600.00

* Increased value recently due to someone 'discovering' five years later that 3.4m mintage is on the low side compared to most other 50p coins. They should only be worth 50p in used condition!

41

COMMEMORATIVE TYPE 17 (Olympic 1)
50 PENCE
Swimmer
(London 2012 Olympics - Aquatics)
Design by: Jonathan Olliffe
Obverse: 4

		UNC	BU
2011	2,179,000	£1.00	£3.00
	Specimen sealed on card		£6.00

Withdrawn coin. Error - lines on face etc, right image £1000.00*

* The actual error coin in the picture above was sold by Rotographic on 27th February 2014 to the highest bidder for £908.88. Not very many are known so the values are likely to vary, as and when they come up for sale. As far as I know, this is one of the highest values on record for a decimal base metal coin. Note that I've also seen a normal coins that someone had manipulated by scratching lines on the face in attempt to pass off as the withdrawn coin!

COMMEMORATIVE TYPE 18 (Olympic 2)
50 PENCE
Hand Pulling an Arrow
(London 2012 Olympics - Archery)
Design by: Piotr Powaga
Obverse: 4

		UNC	BU
2011	3,345,500	£1.00	£3.00
	Specimen sealed on card		£4.00

COMMEMORATIVE TYPE 19 (Olympic 3)
50 PENCE
An Olympic High Jumper - Obverse dated 2011
(London 2012 Olympics - Athletics, see also Commemorative type 14)
Design by: Florence Jackson (aged 8)
Obverse: 4

			UNC	BU
2011	2,224,000	Used: £2.00	£4.00	£5.00
	Specimen sealed on card			£6.00

COMMEMORATIVE TYPE 20 (Olympic 4)
50 PENCE
Shuttlecock
(London 2012 Olympics - Badminton)
Design by: Emma Kelly
Obverse: 4

		UNC	BU
2011	2,133,500	£1.00	£3.00
	Specimen sealed on card		£4.00

COMMEMORATIVE TYPE 21 (Olympic 5)
50 PENCE
Players on Ball-Textured Background
(London 2012 Olympics - Basketball)
Design by: Sarah Payne
Obverse: 4

			UNC	BU
2011	1,748,000	Used: £1.00	£5.00	£10.00
	Specimen sealed on card in undamaged plastic			£30.00
	.925 Silver Proof - See note, page 51			£20.00

COMMEMORATIVE TYPE 22 (Olympic 6)
50 PENCE
Player
(London 2012 Olympics - Boccia)
Design by: Justin Chung
Obverse: 4

		UNC	BU
2011	2,166,000	£1.00	£3.00
	Specimen sealed on card		£4.00

Note: Any Olympic 50p coin can potentially sell for slightly more than face value in used condition, as lots of people are still collecting them and some are willing to pay a bit more.

COMMEMORATIVE TYPE 23 (Olympic 7)
50 PENCE
Boxing Gloves with Ring Ropes
(London 2012 Olympics - Boxing)
Design by: Shane Abery
Obverse: 4

		UNC	BU
2011	2,148,500	£1.00	£3.00
	Specimen sealed on card		£4.00

COMMEMORATIVE TYPE 24 (Olympic 8)
50 PENCE
Canoeist in Choppy Waters
(London 2012 Olympics - Canoeing)
Design by: Timothy Lees
Obverse: 4

		UNC	BU
2011	2,166,000	£1.00	£3.00
	Specimen sealed on card		£4.00

COMMEMORATIVE TYPE 25 (Olympic 9)
50 PENCE
Cyclist
(London 2012 Olympics - Cycling)
Design by: Theo Crutchley-Mack
Obverse: 4

		UNC	BU
2011	2,090,500	£1.00	£3.00
	Specimen sealed on card		£4.00
	.925 Silver Proof - See note, page 51		£20.00

COMMEMORATIVE TYPE 26 (Olympic 10)
50 PENCE
Horse, Jumping
(London 2012 Olympics - Equestrian)
Design by: Thomas Babbage
Obverse: 4

		UNC	BU
2011	2,142,500	£1.00	£3.00
	Specimen sealed on card		£5.00

COMMEMORATIVE TYPE 27 (Olympic 11)
50 PENCE
Fencing
(London 2012 Olympics - Fencing)
Design by: Ruth Summerfield
Obverse: 4

		UNC	BU
2011	2,115,500	£1.00	£3.00
	Specimen sealed on card		£4.00

COMMEMORATIVE TYPE 28 (Olympic 12)
OFFSIDE EXPLAINED / 50 PENCE
Diagram of the Offside Rule
(London 2012 Olympics - Football)
Design by: Neil Wolfson
Obverse: 4

		Used	BU
2011	1,125,500	£4.00	£8.00
	Specimen sealed on card		£12.00

Note: Any Olympic 50p coin can potentially sell for slightly more than face value in used condition, as lots of people are still collecting them and some are willing to pay a bit more.

COMMEMORATIVE TYPE 29 (Olympic 13)
50 PENCE
Player with Ball
(London 2012 Olympics - Goalball)
Design by: Jonathan Wren
Obverse: 4

		UNC	BU
2011	1,615,500	£1.00	£3.00
	Specimen sealed on card		£5.00

COMMEMORATIVE TYPE 30 (Olympic 14)
50 PENCE
Gymnast
(London 2012 Olympics - Gymnastics)
Design by: Jonathan Olliffe
Obverse: 4

		UNC	BU
2011	1,720,813	£1.00	£3.00
	Specimen sealed on card		£5.00

COMMEMORATIVE TYPE 31 (Olympic 15)
50 PENCE
Player with Ball
(London 2012 Olympics - Handball)
Design by: Natasha Ratcliffe
Obverse: 4

		UNC	BU
2011	1,676,500	£1.00	£5.00
	Specimen sealed on card		£9.00

COMMEMORATIVE TYPE 32 (Olympic 16)
50 PENCE
Two Hockey Players
(London 2012 Olympics - Hockey)
Design by: Robert Evans
Obverse: 4

		UNC	BU
2011	1,773,500	£1.00	£3.00
	Specimen sealed on card		£5.00

COMMEMORATIVE TYPE 33 (Olympic 17)
50 PENCE
Judo Throw
(London 2012 Olympics - Judo)
Design by: David Cornell
Obverse: 4

		Used	BU
2011	1,161,500	£4.00	£6.00
	Specimen sealed on card		£8.00

COMMEMORATIVE TYPE 34 (Olympic 18)
50 PENCE
Swimmer and four Silhouettes
(London 2012 Olympics - Modern Pentathlon)
Design by: Daniel Brittain
Obverse: 4

		UNC	BU
2011	1,689,500	£1.00	£3.00
	Specimen sealed on card		£5.00

Note: Any Olympic 50p coin can potentially sell for slightly more than face value in used condition, as lots of people are still collecting them and some are willing to pay a bit more.

COMMEMORATIVE TYPE 35 (Olympic 19)
50 PENCE
Slogans and Two Rowers
(London 2012 Olympics - Rowing)
Design by: Davey Podmore
Obverse: 4

		UNC	BU
2011	1,717,300	£1.00	£3.00
	Specimen sealed on card		£5.00

COMMEMORATIVE TYPE 36 (Olympic 20)
50 PENCE
Sailing Boats on the Sea
(London 2012 Olympics - Sailing)
Design by: Bruce Rushin
Obverse: 4

		UNC	BU
2011	1,749,500	£1.00	£3.00
	Specimen sealed on card		£5.00

COMMEMORATIVE TYPE 37 (Olympic 21)
50 PENCE
Figure, Shooting
(London 2012 Olympics - Shooting)
Design by: Pravin Dewdhory
Obverse: 4

		UNC	BU
2011	1,656,500	£1.00	£3.00
	Specimen sealed on card		£5.00

COMMEMORATIVE TYPE 38 (Olympic 22)
50 PENCE
Table Tennis Bats, Ball etc
(London 2012 Olympics - Table Tennis)
Design by: Alan Linsdell
Obverse: 4

		UNC	BU
2011	1,737,500	£1.00	£3.00
	Specimen sealed on card		£5.00

COMMEMORATIVE TYPE 39 (Olympic 23)
50 PENCE
Two Figures Participating in Taekwando
(London 2012 Olympics - Taekwando)
Design by: David Gibbons
Obverse: 4

		UNC	BU
2011	1,664,000	£1.00	£4.00
	Specimen sealed on card		£5.00

COMMEMORATIVE TYPE 40 (Olympic 24)
50 PENCE
Tennis Ball and Net
(London 2012 Olympics - Tennis)
Design by: Tracy Baines
Obverse: 4

		UNC	BU	Proof
2011	1,454,000	£1.00	£3.00	
	Specimen sealed on card		£5.00	
2012	Also exists dated 2012, struck as a gold piedfort proof			£3,000

Note: Any Olympic 50p coin can potentially sell for slightly more than face value in used condition, as lots of people are still collecting them and some are willing to pay a bit more.

COMMEMORATIVE TYPE 4I (Olympic 25)
50 PENCE
Silhouettes of Runner, Cyclist and Swimmer
(London 2012 Olympics - Triathlon)
Design by: Sarah Harvey
Obverse: 4

		Used	BU
2011	1,163,500	£5.50	£7.00
	Specimen sealed on card		£12.00

COMMEMORATIVE TYPE 42 (Olympic 26)
50 PENCE
Three Players and Central Net
(London 2012 Olympics - Volleyball)
Design by: Daniela Boothman
Obverse: 4

		UNC	BU
2011	2,133,500	£1.00	£3.00
	Specimen sealed on card		£5.00

COMMEMORATIVE TYPE 43 (Olympic 27)
50 PENCE
Basic Outline of a Weightlifter
(London 2012 Olympics - Weightlifting)
Design by: Rob Shakespeare
Obverse: 4

		UNC	BU
2011	1,879,000	£1.00	£3.00
	Specimen sealed on card		£4.00

Note: Any Olympic 50p coin can potentially sell for slightly more than face value in used condition, as lots of people are still collecting them and some are willing to pay a bit more.

COMMEMORATIVE TYPE 44 (Olympic 28)
50 PENCE
Man Playing, Ball in Lap
(London 2012 Olympics - Wheelchair Rugby)
Design by: Natasha Ratcliffe
Obverse: 4

		UNC	BU
2011	1,765,500	£1.00	£3.00
	Specimen sealed on card		£5.00
	.925 Silver Proof - See note, page 51		£20.00

COMMEMORATIVE TYPE 45 (Olympic 29)
50 PENCE
Wrestlers
(London 2012 Olympics - Wrestling)
Design by: Roderick Enriquez
Obverse: 4

		Used	BU
2011	1,129,500	£3.00	£6.00
	Specimen sealed on card		£8.00

Olympic 30
Medallion Only
The Royal Mint issued a medallion with the 29x 50p coins. It's not a coin, but is mentioned here for completeness. Values are around £30 - £40.
Similar 'completer' medals were issued later with a different non Olympic design and are usually cheaper.

The 50p Olympic Coins - Silver Proofs

Noted so far in silver proof form are: Basketball, Cycling and Wheelchair Rugby. The Royal Mint apparently also made three 'sets' of six silver proof coins which included the Fencing, Badminton, Basketball, Hockey, Tennis and the, I quote, 'wildly popular' football coin!

Gold Versions: Gold proofs were struck by the Royal Mint and just given to the designers of the coins. They are therefore extremely rare!

27.3 mm • 8.0 grammes • cupro-nickel • plain edge

COMMEMORATIVE TYPE 46

FIFTY PENCE / 50

Ironside's rejected design for the original 1969 50p
(This is what the original Britannia 50p could have looked like)
Design by: Christopher Ironside
Obverse: 4

		UNC	BU	Proof
2013	7,000,000	£1.00	£4.00	£10.00
4,403	Specimen in folder		£20.00	
1,823 of 4.5k	.925 sterling silver proof			£50.00
816 of 1,500	.925 sterling silver piedfort proof			£80.00
198 of 340	.917 gold proof, price new			£700.00

COMMEMORATIVE TYPE 47

BENJAMIN / COMPOSER BORN 1913 / BRITTEN

His name in a double stave,
'Blow Bugle blow' and 'Set the
wild echoes flying'.
(To mark the centenary of the birth
of Benjamin Britten)
Design by: Tom Phillips

		UNC	BU	Proof
2013	5,300,000	£1.00	£4.00	£10.00
13,337	Specimen in folder (inc coins sold with stamps)		£9.00	
717 of 2k	.925 sterling silver proof*			£200.00
515 of 1000	.925 sterling silver piedfort proof			£280.00
70 of 150	.917 gold proof, price new			£700.00

*The relatively low silver proof mintage combined with some hype caused this one to rise in value in 2016. People are also asking silly prices for the normal circulation coin as a result!

COMMEMORATIVE TYPE 48

XX / COMMONWEALTH GAMES GLASGOW / 2014

Male cyclist and female runner
(To commemorate the 20th Commonwealth
Games)
Design by: Alex Loudon and Dan Flashman

		UNC	BU	Proof
2014	6,500,000	£1.00	£4.00	£15.00
	Specimen in folder, price new		£10.00	
2500 max	.925 sterling silver proof, price new			£50.00
1000 max	.925 sterling silver piedfort proof, price new			£100.00
260 max	.917 gold proof, price new			£725.00

COMMEMORATIVE TYPE 49a
THE BATTLE OF BRITAIN 1940
WITHOUT DENOMINATION
(Pilots scrambling, planes in flight above)
Design by: Gary Breeze
Obverse: 4
(Ian Rank-Broadley portrait, as shown)

Note that the denomination is omitted on all coins with the Ian Rank-Broadley portrait (from the 2015 dated sets), shown here. Apparently deliberate, but I'm sure this was actually an oversight! Confusingly, silver proof and silver piedfort proofs also exist, originally only as part of sets made early in 2015.

		UNC	BU	Proof
2015	(4th portrait, originally in sets only)	£4.00	£10.00	£15.00
	Specimen in folder, price new		£10.00	
1500 max	.925 sterling silver proof, only available in sets of 5x 2015 coins			£75.00?
1500 max	.925 sterling silver piedfort proof, only available in sets as above			£100.00?

COMMEMORATIVE TYPE 49b
THE BATTLE OF BRITAIN 1940
ALSO WITHOUT DENOMINATION
Precious metal proofs only, reverse as 49a
(Jody Clark portrait, no denomination, as shown)

Bizarrely the main precious metal proof coins have the new portrait, but are also missing the denomination!

		Proof
2015	(5th portrait, precious metal proofs only)	
4000 max	.925 sterling silver proof, price new	£50.00
1940 max	.925 sterling silver piedfort proof, price new	£100.00
500 max	.917 gold proof, price new	£675.00

COMMEMORATIVE TYPE 49c
THE BATTLE OF BRITAIN 1940
WITH DENOMINATION
Circulation issue, reverse as 49a
(Jody Clark portrait, with '50 PENCE', as shown)

For circulation issues the Royal Mint released these coins, which not only have the new Jody Clark 5th portrait of the Queen, they also have the denomination written as '50 PENCE' on the obverse.

	UNC
2015 5,900,000 (5th portrait with '50 PENCE')	£2.00

53

27.3 mm • 8.0 grammes • cupro-nickel • plain edge

BATTLE OF HASTINGS / 1066 / 2016
(Representation of a soldier inspired by the Bayeux Tapestry)
Design by: John Bergdahl

		UNC	BU	Proof
2016	6,100,000	£2.00	£5.00	£16.00
	Specimen in folder, price new		£10.00	
3,000 max	.925 sterling silver proof, price new			£50.00
1500 max	.925 sterling silver piedfort proof, price new			£95.00
350 max	.917 gold proof, price new			£785.00

BEATRIX POTTER SERIES No.1, BEATRIX POTTER
(Silhouette of Beatrix Potter, name, dates and Peter Rabbit character shown below)
Design by: Emma Noble

		UNC	BU	Proof
2016	5,000,000	£2.00	£5.00	
	Specimen in pack, price new		£10.00	
	.925 sterling silver proof			£120.00
	.925 sterling silver piedfort proof			£135.00
	.917 gold proof			£650.00

BEATRIX POTTER SERIES, No.2, PETER RABBIT
(The character Peter Rabbit, his name either side)
Design by: Emma Noble
Silver proof colour version shown
Obverse: As Type 51

		UNC	BU	Proof
2016	5,000,000 Standard, non-coloured coin	£1.00	£5.00	
	Standard, non-coloured coin. Extra left whisker, (die damage). **Used:** £3.00			
	Standard, non-coloured coin in pack			£12.00
15,000	.925 coloured sterling silver proof in clear Perspex box			£360.00
500	.925 coloured sterling silver proof in First Day Cover envelope			£300.00
250	.925 coloured sterling silver proof in black box (from Potter shops)			£500+
250	.925 coloured sterling silver proof in cherry box + extras			£500+?

The silver proof Peter Rabbit coins sold incredibly well from the word go. So successful in fact, that despite the coins all being the same, the type of packaging and even the serial number (some people prefer very low numbers) can play a role with values! There are some variations to the values, which seem to be down to the mood of buyers and the number on offer.

54

COMMEMORATIVE TYPE 53
BEATRIX POTTER SERIES, No. 3,
JEMIMA PUDDLE-DUCK
(The character Jemina Puddle-Duck, her name either side**)
Design by: Emma Noble
Obverse: As Type 51

		UNC	BU	Proof
2016	2,100,000 Standard, non-coloured coin	£1.00	£5.00	
	Standard, non-coloured coin in pack		£12.00	
15,000	.925 sterling silver proof in clear Perspex box			£65.00
250	.925 sterling silver proof in black box			£90.00

COMMEMORATIVE TYPE 54
BEATRIX POTTER SERIES, No. 4,
SQUIRREL NUTKIN
(The character Squirrel Nutkin, his name either side**)
Design by: Emma Noble
Obverse: As Type 51

		BU	Proof
2016	3,800,000 Standard, non-coloured coin*	£10.00	
	Standard, non-coloured coin in pack	£12.00	
15,000	.925 sterling silver proof in clear Perspex box		£60.00
250	.925 sterling silver proof in black box		£90.00

* Not yet in circulation at time of writing.

COMMEMORATIVE TYPE 55
BEATRIX POTTER SERIES, No.5,
MRS TIGGY-WINKLE
(The character Mrs Tiggy-Winkle, her name either side**)
Design by: Emma Noble
Obverse: As Type 51

		UNC	BU	Proof
2016	5,700,000 Standard, non-coloured coin	£1.00	£5.00	
	Standard, non-coloured coin in pack		£12.00	
15,000	.925 sterling silver proof in clear Perspex box			£65.00
250	.925 sterling silver proof in black box			£85.00

**All images on this page show the silver proof colour versions of the coins.

COMMEMORATIVE TYPE 56
TEAM GB
(Swimmer, Team GB logo and Olympic rings)
Design by: Tim Sharp
Obverse: As Type 51

		UNC	BU	Proof
2016	6,100,000	£1.00	£4.00	
	Specimen in folder, price new		£5.00	
4,000 max.	.925 sterling silver proof, price new			£60.00
2,016 max.	.925 sterling silver piedfort proof, price new			£95.00
306 max.	.917 gold proof			£800.00

COMMEMORATIVE TYPE 57
SIR ISAAC NEWTON
[Rings and ellipses around the sun /
SIR ISAAC NEWTON above, FIFTY PENCE
below]
Design by: Aaron West

		BU	Proof
2017	Currently only in sets.	£10.00	£10.00
	Specimen in folder, price new	TBC	
	.925 sterling silver proof, price new		TBC
	.925 sterling silver piedfort proof, price new		TBC
	.917 gold proof		TBC

INFO

The "straight" edges of the 50p (and
the 20p) are not flat, but arced to form a Reuleaux
polygon. Any point on an arced
edge is an equal distance from the opposing
vertex. This design enables the coins to
be used in vending machines.

What's currently legal tender?

All £1 coins are legal tender. The £1 coin is the most commonly forged coin, with estimates of between 2-3% of the total £1 coins in circulation being forgeries. Look out for poor definition and mismatching edges or reverses (i.e. a Welsh reverse with a date that should have an English obverse, and/or a coin with edge lettering that doesn't match the country represented on its reverse). If someone gives you a fake £1 coin, you are not legally obliged to accept it.

Correct edge lettering for the year and what they mean

The following coins have the edge inscription DECUS ET TUTAMEN (Latin for 'An ornament and a safeguard'):

1983 (UK theme), 1986 (NI theme), 1987 (English theme), 1988 (UK theme), 1991 (NI theme), 1992 (English theme), 1993 (UK theme), 1996 (NI theme), 1997 (English theme), 1998 (UK theme), 2001 (NI theme), 2002 (English theme), 2003 (UK theme), 2008 (UK theme) and the standard definitive shield reverse coins made from 2008 to 2016 The 2013 English floral theme coin, the 2014 Northern Ireland floral theme coin as well as the 2015 Royal Arms coin and the 2016 Heraldic last round pound also carry the DECUS ET TUTAMEN edge inscription.

Scottish theme coins (dated 1984, 1989, 1994, 1999 and 2014) have the inscription 'NEMO ME IM-PUNE LACESSIT' (Latin for 'No-one provokes me with impunity').

Welsh theme coins (dated 1985, 1990, 1995, 2000 and 2013) have the inscription 'PLEIDIOL WYF I'M GWLAD' (Welsh for 'True I am to my country').

The bridge themed coins (dated 2004, 2005, 2006 and 2007) have a patterned edge with no edge lettering.

The capital city themed coins have the following edge inscriptions:

2010, Belfast - 'PRO TANTO QUID RETRIBUAMUS' (what shall we give in return for so much).
2010, London - 'DOMINE DIRIGE NOS' (Lord, direct us).
2011, Cardiff - 'Y DDRAIS GOCH DDYRY CYCHWYN' (the red dragon inspires action).
2011, Edinburgh - 'NISI DOMINUS FRUSTRA' (without the Lord, in vain)

Which are hard to find?

The hardest £1 coins to find in circulation are 1998 and 1999 as they were only made for year sets. The 1988 has a popular design and relatively low mintage of just over seven million which doesn't make it rare, but it's certainly the scarcest in comparison to most of the other earlier coins. The 2011 Edinburgh coin has a mintage of under one million and often sells for more than face value, even in used condition.

The 2016 Heraldic beast 'last round pound' coin appeared in sets and special packaging only, so the mintage of this one should also be fairly low.

OBVERSES

OBVERSE 1
(used 1983 & 1984)
D•G•REG•F•D•(date) || ELIZABETH II
Elizabeth II, Dei Gratia Regina, Fidei Defensor
(Elizabeth II, By the Grace of God Queen and Defender of the Faith)
Portrait by: Arnold Machin

OBVERSE 2
(used 1985 - 1997)
ELIZABETH II || D•G•REG•F•D•(date)
Elizabeth II, Dei Gratia Regina, Fidei Defensor
(Elizabeth II, By the Grace of God Queen and Defender of the Faith)
Portrait by: Raphael Maklouf

OBVERSE 3
(used 1998 - 2008)
ELIZABETH II•D•G || REG•F•D•(date)
Elizabeth II, Dei Gratia Regina, Fidei Defensor
(Elizabeth II, By the Grace of God Queen and Defender of the Faith)
Portrait by: Ian Rank-Broadley

OBVERSE 4 (similar to last, with no rim beading)
(used 2008 to 2015)
ELIZABETH II•D•G || REG•F•D•(date)
Elizabeth II, Dei Gratia Regina, Fidei Defensor
(Elizabeth II, By the Grace of God Queen and Defender of the Faith)
Portrait by: Ian Rank-Broadley

OBVERSE 5
(used 2015 onwards)
ELIZABETH II•D•G || REG•F•D•(date)
Elizabeth II, Dei Gratia Regina, Fidei Defensor
(Elizabeth II, By the Grace of God Queen and Defender of the Faith)
Portrait by: Jody Clark

1983	UK Royal Arms design by Eric Sewell Edge: DECUS ET TUTAMEN			
		UNC	BU	Proof
443,053,510		£2.50	£5.00	£5.00
484,900	Specimen in folder		£6.00	
50,000	.925 sterling silver proof			£25.00
10,000	.925 sterling silver piedfort proof			£60.00

The following 4 coins ("Coronet" series) were designed by Leslie Durbin.

1984	Scottish Thistle in Coronet. Edge: NEMO ME IMPUNE LACESSIT			
146,256,501		£3.00	£5.00	£5.00
27,960	Specimen in folder		£6.00	
44,855	.925 sterling silver proof			£20.00
15,000	.925 sterling silver piedfort proof			£30.00

1985	Welsh Leek in Coronet. Edge: PLEIDIOL WYF I'M GWLAD			
228,430,749		£3.00	£5.00	£5.00
24,850	Specimen in folder		£6.00	
50,000	.925 sterling silver proof			£20.00
15,000	.925 sterling silver piedfort proof			£30.00

1986	N.I. Flax in Coronet. Edge: DECUS ET TUTAMEN			
10,409,501		£3.00	£5.00	£5.00
19,908	Specimen in folder		£6.00	
37,958	.925 sterling silver proof			£20.00
15,000	.925 sterling silver piedfort proof			£30.00

1987	English Oak in Coronet. Edge: DECUS ET TUTAMEN			
39,298,502		£3.00	£5.00	£5.00
72,607	Specimen in folder		£6.00	
50,500	.925 sterling silver proof			£20.00
15,000	.925 sterling silver piedfort proof			£30.00

1988   Royal Shield design (UK) by Derek Gorringe
Edge: DECUS ET TUTAMEN

		UNC	BU	Proof
7,118,825	Used: £1.50	£3.00	£8.00	£10.00
29,550	Specimen in folder		£10.00	
50,000	.925 sterling silver proof			£25.00
10,000	.925 sterling silver piedfort proof			£30.00

The following 4 coins ("Coronet" series) were designed by Leslie Durbin.

1989   Scottish Thistle in Coronet.
Edge: NEMO ME IMPUNE LACESSIT

70,580,501		£3.00	£5.00	£5.00
25,000	.925 sterling silver proof			£20.00
10,000	.925 sterling silver piedfort proof			£30.00

1990   Welsh Leek in Coronet. Edge: PLEIDIOL WYF I'M GWLAD

97,269,302		£3.00	£5.00	£5.00
25,000	.925 sterling silver proof			£20.00

1991   N.I. Flax in Coronet. Edge: DECUS ET TUTAMEN

38,443,575		£3.00	£5.00	£8.00
25,000	.925 sterling silver proof			£20.00

1992   English Oak in Coronet. Edge: DECUS ET TUTAMEN

36,320,487		£3.00	£5.00	£5.00
25,000	.925 sterling silver proof			£20.00

1993 UK Royal Arms design by Eric Sewell
Edge: DECUS ET TUTAMEN

		UNC	BU	Proof
114,744,500		£3.00	£5.00	£5.00
50,000	.925 sterling silver proof			£20.00
10,000	.925 sterling silver piedfort proof			£30.00

The following 4 coins ("Heraldic" series) were designed by Norman Sillman.

1994 Scottish Lion Rampant. Edge: NEMO ME IMPUNE LACESSIT

29,752,525		£2.00	£5.00	£7.00
	Specimen in folder		£5.00	
25,000	.925 sterling silver proof			£20.00
11,722	.925 sterling silver piedfort proof			£30.00

1995 Welsh Dragon. Edge: PLEIDIOL WYF I'M GWLAD

34,503,501		£2.00	£5.00	£7.00
	Specimen in folder		£5.00	
	Specimen in folder (Welsh text)		£8.00	
27,445	.925 sterling silver proof			£20.00
8,458	.925 sterling silver piedfort proof			£30.00

1996 N.I. Celtic Cross. Edge: DECUS ET TUTAMEN

89,886,000		£2.00	£5.00	£7.00
	Specimen in folder		£5.00	
25,000	.925 sterling silver cased proof			£20.00
10,000	.925 sterling silver piedfort cased proof			£30.00

1997 English Three Lions. Edge: DECUS ET TUTAMEN

57,117,450		£2.00	£5.00	£7.00
	Specimen in folder		£5.00	
20,137	.925 sterling silver proof			£20.00
10,000	.925 sterling silver piedfort proof			£30.00

1998 UK Royal Arms design by Eric Sewell
Edge: DECUS ET TUTAMEN

		UNC	BU	Proof
(BU packs only)			£14.00	£15.00
13,843	.925 sterling silver proof			£25.00
10,000	.925 sterling silver piedfort proof			£35.00

1999 Scottish Lion Rampant. Edge: NEMO ME IMPUNE LACESSIT

		UNC	BU	Proof
(BU packs only)			£14.00	£15.00
25,000	.925 sterling silver proof			£25.00
2,000	.925 sterling "Special Frosted Finish" proof			£35.00
10,000	.925 sterling silver piedfort proof			£35.00

2000 Welsh Dragon. Edge: PLEIDIOL WYF I'M GWLAD

		UNC	BU	Proof
109,496,500		£2.00	£5.00	£7.00
40,000	.925 sterling silver proof			£25.00
2,000	.925 sterling "Special Frosted Finish" proof			£35.00
10,000	.925 sterling silver piedfort proof			£35.00

2001 N.I. Celtic Cross. Edge: DECUS ET TUTAMEN

		UNC	BU	Proof
58,093,731		£2.00	£5.00	£7.00
13,237	.925 sterling silver proof			£25.00
2,000	.925 sterling "Special Frosted Finish" proof			£35.00
8,464	.925 sterling silver piedfort proof			£35.00

2002 English Three Lions. Edge: DECUS ET TUTAMEN

		UNC	BU	Proof
77,818,000		£2.00	£5.00	£7.00
17,693	.925 sterling silver proof			£25.00
2,000	.925 sterling "Special Frosted Finish" proof			£35.00
6,599	.925 sterling silver piedfort proof			£35.00

2003 UK Royal Arms design by Eric Sewell
Edge: DECUS ET TUTAMEN

		UNC	BU	Proof
61,596,500		£2.00	£5.00	£10.00
15,830	.925 sterling silver proof			£25.00
9,871	.925 sterling silver piedfort proof			£35.00

2003 dated Bridges 'PATTERN' set of 4 coins (one shown to left)
7,500 max .925 sterling silver proofs, edge hallmarked   £70.00
3,000 max .917 gold proofs, edge hall marked   £2000.00

2004 dated Heraldic beasts 'PATTERN' set of 4 coins (proof only)
5,000 max .925 sterling silver proofs, edge hallmarked   £90.00
2,250 max .917 gold proofs, edge hallmarked   £2100.00

The following 4 coins ("Bridge" series) were designed by Edwina Ellis. The edges all feature a decorative pattern.

2004	Scotland - Forth Bridge	UNC	BU	Proof
39,162,000		£3.00	£6.00	£9.00
24,014	Specimen in folder		£30.00	
11,470	.925 sterling silver proof			£25.00
7,013	.925 sterling silver piedfort cased proof			£35.00
2,618	.917 gold proof			£500.00

2005	Wales - Menai Bridge	UNC	BU	Proof
99,429,500		£3.00	£6.00	£9.00
24,802	Specimen in folder		£20.00	
8,371	.925 sterling silver proof			£25.00
6,007	.925 sterling silver piedfort cased proof			£40.00
1,195	.917 gold proof			£500.00

2006	Northern Ireland - Egyptian Arch	UNC	BU	Proof
38,938,000		£3.00	£6.00	£9.00
23,856	Specimen in folder		£20.00	
14,765	.925 sterling silver proof			£28.00
5,129	.925 sterling silver piedfort cased proof			£40.00
728	.917 gold proof			£550.00

2007	England - Millennium Bridge	UNC	BU	Proof
26,180,160		£3.00	£6.00	£9.00
5,326	Specimen in folder		£20.00	
10,110	.925 sterling silver proof			£28.00
5,739	.925 sterling silver piedfort cased proof			£40.00
1,122	.917 gold proof			£550.00

22.5 mm • 9.5 grammes • nickel-brass • lettered edge

2008   UK Royal Arms design by: Eric Sewell. With Obverse 3.
Edge: DECUS ET TUTAMEN

		UNC	BU	Proof
3,910,000		£2.00	£4.00	£8.00
9,134	.925 sterling silver proof			£30.00
7,894	.925 sterling silver piedfort cased proof			£45.00
2,005	Set of 14 £1 coins, all designs 1983 - 2008. Silver with gold coloured 'silhouette' details. All dated 2008			£300.00
	As above, as gold proof set			-

Large shield part of the UK Royal coat of Arms by:
Matthew Dent. With Obverse 4 or 5. Struck annually.

2008	43,827,300	£2.00	£4.00	£10.00
5,000	.925 sterling silver proof			£30.00
2,456	.925 sterling piedfort proof			£50.00
860	.917 gold proof			£600.00
2009				
	27,625,600	£2.00	£4.00	£10.00
	.925 sterling silver proof from set			£30.00
	.917 gold proof			£600.00
2010	57,120,000	£2.00	£4.00	£10.00
2011	25,415,000	£2.00	£5.00	£10.00
2012	35,700,030	£2.00	£5.00	£10.00
	.925 sterling silver proof (1234 sold)			£20.00
2013	13,090,500	£2.00	£6.00	£10.00
	.925 sterling silver proof			£40.00
	.917 gold proof (17 sold, plus 59 in sets)			-
2014	79,305,200	£2.00	£6.00	£10.00
2015	29,580,000 (Obverse 4)	£2.00	£6.00	£10.00
2015	(Obverse 5) (available in sets only) *		£10.00	£10.00
2016	Available in sets only		£10.00	£12.00

* A mintage figure of 62,745,640 is currently quoted for this coin on the Royal Mint website. It's probably wrong. At least, judging by the fact that none are seen in circulated condition indicates to me that they were made for sets only. It is likely that the mintage figure is that of the 2015 Royal Arms coin.

The following 4 coins ("Capital Cities" series) were designed by Stuart Devlin and all use Obverse 4.

2010 Belfast
  Edge: PRO TANTO QUID RETRIBUAMUS

	UNC	BU	Proof
6,205,000	£2.00	£9.00	£9.00
.925 sterling silver proof			£40.00
.925 sterling silver piedfort proof			£80.00

2010 London
  Edge: DOMINE DIRIGE NOS

2,635,000	£2.00	£0.00*	£9.00
.925 sterling silver proof			£40.00
.925 sterling silver piedfort proof			£80.00

* Some of the BU packs contained the 2010 Shield reverse coin in error.

2011 Cardiff
  Edge: Y DDRAIS GOCH DDYRY CYCHWYN

1,615,000	£2.00	£9.00	£12.00
.925 sterling silver proof (5,553 sold)			£40.00
.925 sterling silver piedfort proof (1,615 sold)			£80.00
.917 gold proof (524 sold)			-

2011 Edinburgh
  Edge: NISI DOMINUS FRUSTRA

935,000 Used: £3.00*	£5.00*	£15.00*	£15.00*
.925 sterling silver proof (4,973 sold)			£40.00
.925 sterling silver piedfort proof (2,696 sold)			£60.00
.917 gold proof (499 sold)			-

*Lately higher values than shown due to a fresh wave of tabloid hype. In a perfect world free of media influence and hobby speculators they would be worth £1!

2013	National Floral Symbols series - England, by Timothy Noad Edge: DECUS ET TUTAMEN			
		UNC	BU	Proof
	5,270,000	£2.00	£7.00	£10.00
1,858	.925 sterling silver proof*			£80.00
1,071	.925 sterling silver piedfort proof			£100.00
185	.917 gold proof (plus 99 in sets with Wales)			-

2013	National Floral Symbols series - Wales by Timothy Noad Edge: PLEIDIOL WYF I'M GWLAD			
	5,270,000	£2.00	£7.00	£10.00
1,618	.925 sterling silver proof*			£80.00
860	.925 sterling silver piedfort proof			£100.00
175	.917 gold proof (plus 99 in sets with England)			-

* Plus an additional 1,476 sold in pairs.
? 2013 Silver proof version of the 1988 design   £100.00
? 2013 Silver proof version of the 1983 design   £100.00

2014	National Floral Symbols series - Scotland, by Timothy Noad Edge: NEMO ME IMPUNE LACESSIT			
	5,185,000	£2.00	£7.00	£10.00
	.925 sterling silver proof			£80.00
	.925 sterling silver piedfort proof			£100.00

2014	National Floral Symbols series - N. Ireland, by Timothy Noad Edge: DECUS ET TUTAMEN			
	5,780,000	£2.00	£7.00	£12.00
	.925 sterling silver proof			£80.00
	.925 sterling silver piedfort proof			£100.00

2015   The Royal Arms - by Timothy Noad
Edge: DECUS ET TUTAMEN

		UNC	BU	Proof
All with Obverse 5				
	62,745,640	£2.00	£7.00	
	In card pack, price new		£10.00	
3,500 max	.925 sterling silver proof, price new			£50.00
2,000 max	.925 sterling piedfort proof, price new			£100.00
500 max	.917 gold proof, price new			£850.00

2016   Four Heraldic beast symbols of the UK -
by Gregory Cameron, Bishop of St Asaph.
'The last round pound'. Edge: DECUS ET TUTAMEN

		UNC	BU	Proof
	None circulated, has to be purchased		£10.00	
7,000 max	.925 sterling silver proof			£75.00
4,500 max	.925 sterling piedfort proof			£160.00
500 max	.917 gold proof			£1300.00

Good-bye to the round pound coin.

It is generally well known by now that the round pound coin will be phased-out in 2017. The new 12-sided coin will appear at the end of March and will circulate along-side all the existing round pound coins until October. From October the banks will only pay out the new pound coins and the old ones will cease to be legal tender.

Despite what some elements of the media will lead you to believe - there is no need to panic!

There are so many round pounds coins out there, and perhaps more significantly, there are a huge amount of BU single coins/sets and proof sets containing perfect pound coins from every year since they were first made in 1983. There are and always will be plenty to go round. In fact, if the demonetisation of previous coins is anything to go by, the round pound coins are likely to soon be forgotten about (or at least to be less widely collected than they are now), just like the large sized 50p, 10p and 5p coins that were removed from circulation in the 1990s. The old pound coin is likely to be more popular than the obsolete three denominations mentioned above, simply because there is more design variety and I think that will mean they will be fondly remembered and collected by many for years to come. Lots of people though, are only really interested in collecting coins they can find in their change, which means of course, that they will stop collecting round pounds. Ultimately they will find their own value level and there should (in the long term) be very few, if any, that will be worth more than £1 in normal used battered condition. There is no need to panic buy them in 2017 just because you won't be able to find them in change any more. I expect there'll be thousands available from the all the usual places for many decades to come!

Most importantly; don't believe anything you read in the newspapers or those trashy click-bait articles on the internet regarding coins!

I'm thrilled to introduce:

The Check Your Change App, which is available for Android™ devices on Google Play.

It contains a database of the 347 different coins that can currently be found in circulation, plus a further 43 coins that were only sold in sets or packages, including the coins released so far in 2017. The app is free to download and use.

Features of the free app:

- Mark coins as owned (including the ability to add a quantity).
- Filter by coins you have or coins you need.
- Running total of coins owned out of the possible total made.
- The more valuable/sought after coins have a bronze, silver or gold icon.
- Coins that were only available to purchase are marked clearly with an icon and can be toggled visible or invisible.
- Mintage figures.
- View large images of the coins.
- Add your own notes to every coin (e.g. condition, where you got it etc).
- The app is free of adverts.

Unlock the premium feature (for a small fee) to reveal valuations for each coin in both 'Used' and 'As New' condition. The valuations within an app have the advantage that they can be updated a lot easier than in a printed book and the small fee includes free price updates for one year.

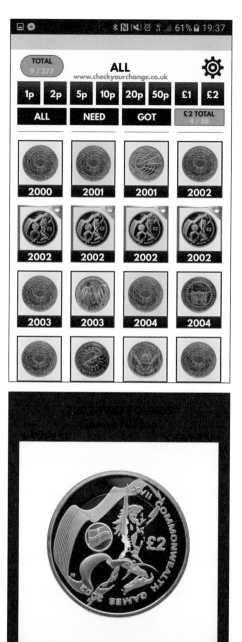

Screenshots showing:

Left - The main coin summary page with the £2 denomination selected.

Below - The individual coin page for the 2014 Glasgow Games 50p with valuations unlocked.

Below left - A fully enlarged 2002 Commonwealth Games 2002 £2 image.

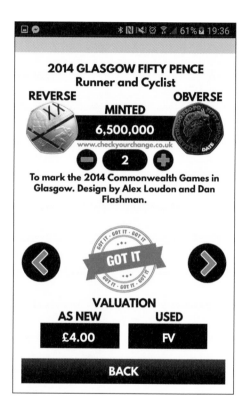

The New Twelve-Sided £1 Coin

On the 19th March 2014 the Chancellor of the Exchequer announced that a completely new £1 coin would be produced to replace the existing type. It is hoped that these will be much harder to counterfeit than the current single-metal round £1 coins, which were struck from 1983 to 2016 and are a target for forgers.

The new 12-sided pound first appeared for sale on the 1st January 2017 within the 2017 BU and proof sets. It is also available in person from the Royal Mint Experience.

Specifications of the new £1 coin:

Diameter: 23.03mm flat to opposing flat, 23.43mm point to opposing point.
Weight: 8.75 grammes.
Alloy: Centre part - Nickel-brass plated in nickel. Outer ring - Nickel brass.
Edge: The edge has alternately milled and plain flat sections.

New £1 Obverse - enlarged

2015 The Royal Mint TRIAL PIECE

These coins were supplied to vending machine companies for testing and calibration purposes. Figures are not known and cannot be confirmed, but it is likely that anywhere between 5,000 to 11,000+ were supplied (but don't hold me to that!). Recent unconfirmed information suggests that around 200,000 were made in total, which does seem rather a lot. Perhaps they will be officially offered for sale at some point. All of the companies that received them were obliged under contract to return them. Some clearly didn't return them as a few have appeared for sale online. These trial coins remain, according to the contract under which they were supplied, the property of the Royal Mint. The legal implications of third party possession of them remains a grey area. Buyer and seller beware!

As these coins were made during early 2015, they feature the 'old' Ian Rank-Broadley bust of the Queen. Later coins feature the new Jody Clark portrait of the Queen. The reverse has the Royal Mint crest with 'The Royal Mint' above and 'TRIAL PIECE' below.

UNC

Mintage number unconfirmed   £180 - £200

The 12-sided new £1 coin - reverse design by David Pearce

In late 2016 I saw pictures of a coin dated 2016 which looked to be authentic and was, according to its owner, found in change. There are also press photographs that clearly show 2016 dated coins, so it is likely these were coins produced at a further stage of development, some being supplied to vending machine companies for further testing. The 2016 coins look identical to the coin that was sold to the public in January 2017, with the exception of the date. It has now been confirmed that the Royal Mint will officially release the 2016 dated coins during 2017, and in large numbers!

		BU	Proof
2016	500,000,000+		
2017	Currently available in sets/packs only	£20.00	£35.00
	.925 sterling silver proof		TBC
	.925 sterling silver piedfort and gold proof		TBC

28.40 mm • 15.98 grammes • nickel-brass • various edges

What's currently legal tender?
All £2 coins dated from 1986 to date are legal tender. The earlier single metal type coins dated 1986 to 1996 are not often seen in circulation and therefore may not be accepted by some merchants who are unfamiliar with them. All of the single metal type coins tend to be worth a little more than face value, even in used condition. Note that there are fake £2 coins in circulation, mostly with recent commemorative designs. They seem to orginate from China.

Which are hard to find?
All of the 1986 to 1996 (single alloy) £2 coins are now hard to find in circulation. The scarcest £2 coin is probably COMMEMORATIVE TYPE 3, the 'Claim of Right' coin, as this was minted in much smaller quantities than the other 1989 £2 coin, and was only issued in Scotland. The bi-metallic coin with the 'Queen wearing a necklace' was never rare. Some of the more recent £2 coins do sell for more than face value, even in used condition! See listings.

COMMEMORATIVE TYPE 1
A thistle encircled by a laurel wreath, superimposed on St. Andrew's Cross
(1986 Commonwealth Games, Edinburgh)
Reverse design by: Norman Sillman
Edge: XIII COMMONWEALTH GAMES SCOTLAND 1986

			UNC	BU	Proof
1986	8,212,184	104,591 Proofs	£5.00	£7.50	£10.00
		Specimen in folder		£8.00	
	58,881	.500 silver UNC	£15.00		
	59,779	.925 sterling silver proof			£22.00
		.917 gold proof			£600.00

COMMEMORATIVE TYPE 2
Intertwined W & M (monogram of William & Mary)
House of Commons Mace, English Crown
TERCENTENARY of the BILL of RIGHTS 1689-1989
Reverse design by: John Lobban
Edge: MILLED

			UNC	BU	Proof
1989	4,432,000	84,704 Proofs	£5.00	£10.00	£10.00
		Partially non frosted proof*			£18.00
		Specimen in folder		£11.00	
	25,000	.925 sterling silver proof			£22.00
	10,000	.925 sterling silver, piedfort proof			£30.00

*Proofs that were part of a Bass Charington promotion appear to have a non frosted bust of the Queen. More comparison is needed at this stage.

COMMEMORATIVE TYPE 3
Intertwined **W & M**
(monogram of William & Mary)
House of Commons Mace, Scottish Crown
TERCENTENARY of the CLAIM of RIGHT
1689-1989
Reverse design by: John Lobban
Edge: MILLED

			Used	UNC	Proof
1989	346,000	84,704 Proofs	£15.00	£20.00	£25.00
		Specimen in folder		£20.00	
		Specimen folder, including both versions ('Bill' & 'Claim')		£30.00	
	24,852	.925 sterling silver proof			£40.00
	10,000	.925 sterling silver, Piedfort proof			£40.00

COMMEMORATIVE TYPE 4
Intertwined **W & M**
(monogram of William & Mary)
Britannia Seated
BANK of ENGLAND 1694-1994
Reverse design by: Leslie Durbin
Edge: SIC VOS NON VOBIS

☆

			UNC	BU	Proof
1994	1,443,116	67,721 Proofs	£6.00	£8.00	£10.00
		Specimen in folder		£9.00	
	27,957	.925 sterling silver proof			£22.00
	9,569	.925 sterling silver, Piedfort proof			£30.00
	1,000	.917 gold proof			£650.00
	? Est. 300	Gold proof mule with wrong obverse*			£2200.00

*The obverse of the double sovereign £2 coin was used in error on some of the gold proof issue. As shown above, the head is larger, legend more abbreviated and it omits the words 'TWO POUNDS'.

COMMEMORATIVE TYPE 5
Dove of Peace
(Commemorating 50 years' peace,
since the end of World War II)
Reverse design by: John Mills
Edge: 1945 IN PEACE GOODWILL 1995

			UNC	BU	Proof
1995	4,388,006	60,639 Proofs	£7.00	£10.00	£10.00
		Specimen in folder		£10.00	
	50,000	.925 sterling silver proof			£22.00
	10,000	.925 sterling silver, Piedfort proof			£30.00
	2,500	.917 gold proof			£600.00

COMMEMORATIVE TYPE 6
UN logo, array of flags
NATIONS UNITED FOR PEACE 1945 - 1995
(50th Anniversary - United Nations)
Reverse design by: Michael Rizzello
Edge: MILLED

			UNC	BU	Proof
1995	Inc. with T5		£9.00	£10.00	£12.00
		Specimen in folder		£15.00	
	175,000	.925 sterling silver proof			£25.00
	10,000	.925 sterling silver Piedfort proof			£30.00
	2,098	.917 gold proof			£600.00

COMMEMORATIVE TYPE 7
Football design, with date, 1996, in centre
(10th European Championship)
Reverse design by: John Mills
Edge: TENTH EUROPEAN CHAMPIONSHIP

			UNC	BU	Proof
1996	5,141,350		£7.50	£9.00	£10.00
	84,704	Specimen in folder		£9.00	
	50,000	.925 sterling silver proof			£20.00
	10,000	.925 sterling silver, Piedfort proof			£30.00
	2,098	.917 gold proof			£600.00

BI-METALLIC £2 COINS (1997 onwards)

OBVERSES

OBVERSE 1
(dated 1997 only, but actually issued in 1998)
ELIZABETH II DEI GRA REGINA F D
Elizabeth II, Dei Gratia Regina, Fidei Defensor
(Elizabeth II, By the Grace of God Queen and Defender of the Faith)
Portrait by: Raphael Maklouf

OBVERSE 2
(used 1998 to 2015)
(Also used on commemoratives 8 to 17, 19, 21 and 32)
ELIZABETH II DEI GRATIA REGINA FID DEF
Elizabeth II, Dei Gratia Regina, Fidei Defensor
(Elizabeth II, By the Grace of God Queen and Defender of the Faith)
Portrait by: Ian Rank-Broadley

| OBVERSE 2b | OBVERSE 2c | OBVERSE 2d |

Variations of obverse 2 - Some of the later reverse designs don't include a date, the face value or both, so these have been incorporated into the obverse legend.

2b: 'TWO POUNDS' at bottom - was used for Commemorative Types
18, 20, 24, 28, 29, 30, 31 & 33
2c: DATE at bottom - was used for Commemorative Types 22, 23 and 25
2d: 'TWO POUNDS' and DATE at bottom - was used for Commemorative Types 26, 27 & 34

OBVERSES (continued)

OBVERSE 3
(used 2015 onwards)
ELIZABETH II DEI GRA REG FID DEF + date
Elizabeth II, Dei Gratia Regina, Fidei Defensor
(Elizabeth II, By the Grace of God Queen and Defender of the Faith)
Portrait by: Jody Clark

OBVERSE 3b

OBVERSE 3c

OBVERSE 3d

OBVERSE 3e

Variations of obverse 3 - Due to the commemorative reverse designs not stating the face value or already featuring the date, there are currently four variations of Obverse 3.

3b: '2 POUNDS' to the left of the Queen - was used for Commemorative Types 33b, 37, 38 and 39.
3c: With no date - was used for Commemorative Type 36.
3d: 'TWO POUNDS' to the left of the Queen, date above - was used for Commemorative Type 34b
3e: '2 POUNDS' to the left of the Queen, date above - was used for Commemorative Type 41.

STANDARD (non commemorative) REVERSES:

REVERSE 1 (standard non-commemorative reverse)
(used 1997 to 2015)
Rings, representing stages of development:
from centre, outward: IRON AGE, INDUSTRIAL REVOLUTION
(cogs), ELECTRONIC AGE (silicon chips), INTERNET AGE
Edge: STANDING ON THE SHOULDERS OF GIANTS
Design by: Bruce Rushin

REVERSE 2 (standard non-commemorative reverse)
(used 2015 onwards)
Britannia facing left, holding trident.
Edge: QUATUOR MARIA VINDICO (I claim the four seas)
Design by: Anthony Dufort

TRIAL TYPES
Sailing ship, probably representing the Golden Hind
A first Bi-metallic coin trial. Coins are dated 1994 but were actually released in 1998. The coins were all issued in packs which also contain examples of the outer and inner blanks and a nickel-brass ring. The obverse used is a modified OBVERSE 1 - very similar, but the trial obverse actually has a dot instead of a small cross between the 'D' and 'ELIZABETH'. The obverse lettering also appears weaker and slightly thinner than usual.

Edge: DECUS ET TUTAMEN ANNO REGNI XLVI
Value: The bi-metallic pack tends to sell for between £100 and £140.

Single metal £2 trial, dated 1994 and marked 'ROYAL MINT TRIAL'
on both sides, also featuring the ship design.
These are very rare. **Value £500.00 - £2000.00**

DEFINITIVE TYPE 1 (obverse 1, reverse 1)

			UNC	BU	Proof
1997	13,734,625		£3.00	£4.00	£7.50
		Specimen in folder		£9.00	
	29,910	.925 silver proof			£20.00
	10,000	.925 silver piedfort proof			£40.00
	2,482	.917 gold proof			£750.00

DEFINITIVE TYPE 2 (obverse 2, reverse 1)

			UNC	BU	Proof
1998	91,110,375	100,000 proofs	FV	£6.00	£7.50
1999*	38,652,000	Used: FV	£60.00	Not seen!	
2000	25,770,000		FV	£6.00	£7.50
2001	34,984,750		FV	£6.00	£7.50
2002	13,024,750		FV	£6.00	£7.50
2003	17,531,250		FV	£6.00	£7.50
2004	11,981,500		FV	£6.00	£7.50
2005	3,837,250		FV	£6.00	£7.50
2006	16,715,000		FV	£6.00	£7.50
2007	10,270,000		FV	£6.00	£7.50
2008	30,107,000		FV	£6.00	£7.50
2009	8,775,000		FV	£6.00	£7.50
2010	6,890,000		FV	£6.00	£7.50
2011	24,375,030		FV	£6.00	£7.50
2012	3,900,000		FV	£6.00	£7.50
2013	15,860,250		FV	£6.00	£7.50
2014	18,200,000		FV	£6.00	£7.50
2015	35,360,058		FV	£6.00	£7.50

* 1999 was not issued in the proof or BU sets that year and very few people seem to have saved them from change. It is therefore scarce to almost unheard of in top condition, despite the high mintage.

DEFINITIVE TYPE 3 (obverse 3, reverse 2) - The new annual definitive Britannia coin.

				BU	Proof
2015	650,000	Used: £5.00			£14.00
		Specimen in folder, price new	£10.00		
	die alignment error **		£ increasing due to media		
		.917 gold proof, price new			£750.00
2016				£10.00	£15.00
	Not yet known			£10.00	
		.917 gold proof, price new			?

** Some 2015 Britannia £2 coins have been observed with die rotation errors, usually of around 100 - 110 degrees. One has also been observed with die rotation error of about 180 degrees. This error was first made public by me on www.checkyourchange.co.uk in September 2016.

BI-METALLIC COMMEMORATIVE COINS

Note that some Brilliant Uncirculated bi-metallic £2 coins that are still sealed in plastic wrappers can be worth twice or even up to 3x the value shown for BU.

COMMEMORATIVE TYPE 8

Symbolic representation of a stadium with rugby ball and goalposts. '1999' above, 'TWO POUNDS' below
(1999 Rugby World Cup)
Design by: Ron Dutton
Edge: RUGBY WORLD CUP 1999

			UNC	BU	Proof
1999	4,933,000		£3.00	£7.50	£10.00
		Specimen in folder		£15.00	
	9,665	.925 sterling silver proof			£22.00
	10,000	.925 sterling silver hologram Piedfort proof			£75.00
	311	.917 gold proof			£600.00

COMMEMORATIVE TYPE 9

Symbolic representation of Marconi's successful transatlantic wireless transmission of 1901,
'TWO POUNDS' below
Design by: Robert Evans
Edge: WIRELESS BRIDGES THE ATLANTIC...MARCONI 1901...

			UNC	BU	Proof
2001	4,558,000		£3.00	£7.50	£10.00
		Specimen in folder		£15.00	
	11,488	.925 sterling silver proof			£20.00
	6,759	.925 sterling silver Piedfort proof			£30.00
	1,658	.917 gold proof			£600.00

a  b  c  d

COMMEMORATIVE TYPE 10
XVII COMMONWEALTH GAMES 2002
around athlete holding banner, (1 of 4) national flags
(27th Commonwealth Games, Manchester)
Design by: Matthew Bonaccorsi
Edge: SPIRIT OF FRIENDSHIP MANCHESTER 2002

			Used	UNC/BU	Proof
2002	650,500	10a English flag	£6.00	£20/£30	£35.00
	485,500	10b N. Ireland flag	£20.00	£30/£40	£45.00
	771,750	10c Scottish flag	£6.00	£10/£20	£25.00
	588,500	10d Welsh flag	£8.00	£20/£30	£35.00

These coins, being newly 'discovered' as those with the lowest mintages of all the circulating £2 coins tend to sell for more than face value, even in used condition! Certainly worth looking out for in your change, especially the NI coin which looks very similar to the England coin but has a crowned hand in the centre of the flag.

Sets of the 4 Type 10 coins:		Specimens in folder	£100.00	
	47,895	base metal proof set		£100.00
	2,553	.925 sterling silver proof set		£200.00
	3,497	.925 sterling silver Piedfort set (coloured flags)		£350.00
	315	.917 gold proof set		£3,000.00

COMMEMORATIVE TYPE 11
DNA Double Helix pattern, DNA DOUBLE HELIX,
1953 TWO POUNDS 2003
(50th Anniversary - Discovery of DNA)
Design by: John Mills
Edge: DEOXYRIBONUCLEIC ACID

			UNC	BU	Proof
2003	4,299,000		£3.00	£7.50	£10.00
	41,568	Specimen in folder		£15.00	
	11,204	.925 sterling silver proof			£30.00
	8,728	.925 sterling silver Piedfort proof			£40.00
	1,500	.917 gold proof			£570.00

COMMEMORATIVE TYPE 12
Steam locomotive TWO POUNDS R.TREVITHICK
1804 INVENTION INDUSTRY PROGRESS 2004
(200th anniversary - Steam Locomotive)
Design by: Robert Lowe
Edge: pattern of arcs & curves, representing viaducts

			UNC	BU	Proof
2004	5,004,500		£3.00	£7.50	£10.00
	56,871	Specimen in folder		£16.00	
	10,233 of 25k	.925 sterling silver proof			£35.00
	5,303 of 10k	.925 sterling silver Piedfort cased proof			£55.00
	1,500	.917 gold proof			£570.00

COMMEMORATIVE TYPE 13
Swords, Maces, Croziers in a star-burst pattern,
1605-2005, TWO POUNDS
(400th anniversary - Gunpowder Plot)
Design by: Peter Forster
Edge: REMEMBER REMEMBER THE FIFTH OF NOVEMBER*

			UNC	BU	Proof
2005	5,140,500		£3.00	£7.50	£10.00
	47,895	Specimen in folder		£15.00	
	4,394	.925 sterling silver proof			£25.00
	4,584	.925 sterling silver Piedfort proof			£45.00
	914	.917 gold proof			£570.00

* These very often end up having missing tails on the 'R's of the edge lettering, so that they can in extreme cases read PEMEMBEP PEMEMBEP THE FIFTH OF NOVEMBEP. This problem with certain edge letters has also been noted on some other £2 and £1 coins. It makes them a little more interesting, but it is my opinion that such errors should have no real influence on the value. I say should have no real influence on the value, but it seems it can sometimes have an affect on value, at least on eBay, where PEMEMBER coins in normal used condition were once exchanging hands for £10 and examples in UNC or near to UNC condition have been sold in the past for £20 - £30. Judging by the number of them that is constantly available, they should theoretically attract no premium.

INFO

Some £2 coins still sealed in original 'specimen' BU packaging have been known to sell for considerably more than shown.

COMMEMORATIVE TYPE 14
St. Paul's Cathedral, floodlit with spotlights.
1945-2005, TWO POUNDS
(60th anniversary - End of World War II)
Design by: Robert Elderton
Edge: IN VICTORY: MAGNANIMITY, IN PEACE: GOODWILL

			UNC	BU	Proof
2005	10,191,000		£3.00	£8.00	
	53,686	Specimen in folder		£20.00	
	Specimen folder (including special edition medallion)			£25.00	
	21,734	.925 sterling silver proof			£30.00
	Not Known	*Error edge: REMEMBER REMEMBER THE FIFTH OF NOVEMBER .925 silver proof			£400.00?
	4,798	.925 sterling silver Piedfort proof			£45.00
	2,924	.917 gold proof			£570.00

* The error edge 60th Anniversary of the End of WWII £2 coin has obviously ended up with the edge inscription of the other themed £2 coin struck that year to commemorate the gunpowder plot. The author has only been informed of one such coin and was lucky enough to have been given the opportunity to purchase it. There may be other similar errors, (see also Type 18) but so far no other TYPE 14 edge error coins have been reported. This is one of those discoveries that can make new coins interesting! I'd be interested to hear if any other readers come across another example of the error edge inscription coins. Update 2017 no others have been reported in over 7 years.

COMMEMORATIVE TYPE 15
Portrait of Isambard Kingdom Brunel in front of machinery
TWO POUNDS | 2006
(200th anniversary - Birth of Isambard Kingdom Brunel)
Design by: Rod Kelly
Edge: 1806-59 . ISAMBARD KINGDOM BRUNEL . ENGINEER

			UNC	BU	Proof
2006	7,928,250		£3.00	£8.00	£10.00
	54,564	Specimen in folder		£10.00	
	7,251 of 20k	.925 sterling silver proof			£30.00
	3,199 of 5k	.925 sterling silver Piedfort proof			£40.00
	1,071 of 1,500	.917 gold proof			£570.00

Known to exist with its outer ring made from a 206 heroic acts 50p! Believed unique.

The words 'TWO POUNDS' above Mr Brunel on the reverse often looks more like 'TWO DOUNDS', due to the tail of the 'P' being obscured by the join between the inner and outer metal types.

The Brunel coins (types 15 and 16) were also sold in pairs in a folder and also cased as silver proofs.

COMMEMORATIVE TYPE 16
Representation of the engineering achievements of I.K.Brunel,
2006 | BRUNEL | TWO POUNDS
(200th anniversary - Birth of Isambard Kingdom Brunel)
Design by: Robert Evans
Edge: SO MANY IRONS IN THE FIRE

			UNC	BU	Proof
2006	7,452,250		£3.00	£8.00	£10.00
	12,694	Specimen in folder		£15.00	
	5,375 of 20k	.925 sterling silver proof			£30.00
	Not Known	.925 sterling silver proof with no edge lettering			£300.00?
	3,018 of 5k	.925 sterling silver Piedfort proof			£40.00
	746 of 1,500	.917 gold proof			£570.00

COMMEMORATIVE TYPE 17
Jigsaw pieces of the English rose and Scottish thistle,
TWO | 2007 | POUNDS | 1707
(300th anniversary - Act of Union between England and Scotland)
Design by: Yvonne Holton
Edge: UNITED INTO ONE KINGDOM

			UNC	BU	Proof
2007	7,545,000		£3.00	£8.00	£10.00
	8,863	Specimen in folder		£20.00	
	8,310	.925 sterling silver proof			£28.00
	4,000	.925 sterling silver Piedfort proof			£40.00
	750	.917 gold proof			£570.00

COMMEMORATIVE TYPE 18
Five link chain with broken link as the nought in 1807,
AN ACT FOR THE ABOLITION OF THE SLAVE TRADE | 2007
(200th anniversary - Abolition of the British slave trade)
Design by: David Gentleman
Edge: AM I NOT A MAN AND A BROTHER
Obverse: 2b

			UNC	BU	Proof
2007	8,445,000	(no 'DG' initials)	£10.00	Hard to find	
	8,688	Specimen in folder ('DG' to right of chain) £25.00			£10.00
	7,095	.925 sterling silver proof ('DG' to right of chain)			£25.00*
	3,990	.925 sterling silver Piedfort proof			£55.00
	1000 max	.917 gold proof			£570.00

* A proof version of this coin is known to exist with the 'THE 4TH OLYMPIAD LONDON
edge legend, obviously meant for Type 19. See also the note under Type 14.

83

28.40 mm • 12.0 grammes • bi-metal • various edge

COMMEMORATIVE TYPE 19
Running Track
LONDON OLYMPIC CENTENARY | 1908 | TWO POUNDS | 2008
(Centenary - 1908 London Olympics)
Design by: Thomas T Docherty
Edge: THE 4TH OLYMPIAD LONDON
Obverse: 2

			Used	BU	Proof
2008	910,000		£4.00	£20.00	£15.00
	29,594 of 100k	Specimen in folder		£25.00	
	6,841 of 20k	.925 sterling silver proof			£50.00
	1,619 of 2,000	.925 sterling silver Piedfort proof			£75.00
	1,908	.917 gold proof			£600.00

COMMEMORATIVE TYPE 20
Olympic flag and two hands
BEIJING 2008 | LONDON 2012
(Olympic handover ceremony)
Design by: Royal Mint in House
Edge: I CALL UPON THE YOUTH OF THE WORLD
Obverse: 2b

			Used	BU	Proof
2008	918,000		£4.00	£20.00	
	47,765 of 250k	Specimen in folder		£25.00	
	30,000	.925 sterling silver proof			£45.00
	3,000	.925 sterling silver Piedfort proof			£75.00
	3,250	.917 gold proof			£600.00

COMMEMORATIVE TYPE 21
Darwin facing ape
1809 DARWIN 2009 | TWO POUNDS
(200th anniversary - birth of Charles Darwin)
Design by: Suzie Zamit
Edge: ON THE ORIGIN OF SPECIES 1859
Obverse: 2

			UNC	BU	Proof
2009	3,903,000		£3.00	£8.00	£10.00
	119,713 of 25k!	Specimen in folder		£20.00	
	9,357	.925 sterling silver proof			£80.00
	3,282	.925 sterling silver Piedfort proof			£110.00
	1000	.917 gold proof			£600.00

COMMEMORATIVE TYPE 22
Burns quote
1759 ROBERT BURNS 1796 | TWO POUNDS
(250 years anniversary - birth of Robert Burns)
Design by: Royal Mint in House
Edge: SHOULD AULD ACQUAINTANCE BE FORGOT
Obverse: 2c

			Used	BU	Proof
2009	3,253,000		£2.50	£8.00	£15.00
	120,223	Specimen in folder		£20.00	
	9,188	.925 sterling silver proof			£30.00
	3,500	.925 sterling silver Piedfort proof			£95.00
	1000	.917 gold proof			£700.00

COMMEMORATIVE TYPE 23
Nurses hands feeling for a pulse
1820 - FLORENCE NIGHTINGALE - 1910 | TWO POUNDS
(150 years of modern nursing and to the centenary of the
death of Florence Nightingale)
Design by: Gordon Summers
Edge: 150 YEARS OF NURSING
Obverse: 2c

			UNC	BU	Proof
2010	6,175,000		£3.00	£8.00	£10.00
	73,160 of 25k!	Specimen in folder		£18.00	
	5,117 of 20k	.925 sterling silver proof			£50.00
	2,770 of 3,5k	.925 sterling silver Piedfort proof			£120.00
	472 of 1000	.917 gold proof			£700.00

A single metal error in cu-ni of this coin is known to exist.

COMMEMORATIVE TYPE 24
King James' Bible
KING JAMES BIBLE | 1611 - 2011
(400 years anniversary - King James' Bible)
Design by: Paul Stafford & Benjamin Wright
Edge: THE AUTHORISED VERSION
Obverse: 2b

			Used	BU	Proof
2011	975,000		£4.00	£20.00	£25.00
	56,268 of 25k!	Specimen in folder		£40.00	
	4,494 of 20k	.925 sterling silver proof			£60.00
	2,394 of 3,5k	.925 sterling silver Piedfort proof			£110.00
	355 of 1000	.917 gold proof			£900.00

28.40 mm • 12.0 grammes • bi-metal • various edge

COMMEMORATIVE TYPE 25
Mary Rose
THE MARY ROSE | TWO POUNDS
(500 Years - Mary Rose)
Design by: John Bergdahl
Edge: 1511 . YOUR NOBLEST SHIPPE .
Obverse: 2c

			Used	BU	Proof
2011	1,040,000		£4.00	£16.00	£15.00
	53,013 of 25k!	Specimen in folder		£40.00	
	6,618 of 20k	.925 sterling silver proof			£70.00
	2,680 of ?2k	.925 sterling silver Piedfort proof			£120.00
	692 of 1000	.917 gold proof			£800.00

COMMEMORATIVE TYPE 26
Olympic Handover
LONDON 2012 | RIO 2016
(Olympic handover ceremony)
Design by: Jonathan Olliffe
Edge: I CALL UPON THE YOUTH OF THE WORLD
Obverse: 2d

			Used	BU	Proof
2012	845,000		£4.00	£10.00	£15.00
	28,356	Specimen in folder		£25.00	
	3,781 of 12k	.925 sterling silver proof			£100.00
	2000 sold	.925 sterling silver Piedfort proof			£120.00
	771 of 100 max!	.917 gold proof			£900.00

COMMEMORATIVE TYPE 27
Charles Dickens
1812 CHARLES DICKENS 1870
(200th anniversary - birth of Charles Dickens)
Design by: Matthew Dent
Edge: SOMETHING WILL TURN UP
Obverse: 2d

			UNC	BU	Proof
2012	8,190,000		£3.00	£8.00	£10.00
	15,035*	Specimen in folder		£25.00	
	2,631 of 20k	.925 sterling silver proof			£50.00
	1279 of 2000	.925 sterling silver Piedfort proof			£130.00
	202 of 850	.917 gold proof, price new			£900.00

*Plus 7,726 in packages combining stamps with the coin.

COMMEMORATIVE TYPE 28
Underground Roundal
1863 | UNDERGROUND | 2013
(150th anniversary - The London Underground)
Design by: Edwina Ellis
Edge: MIND THE GAP
Obverse: 2b

		Used	BU	Proof
2013	1,560,000	£3.00	£15.00	£15.00
	11,647 pairs of coins* Type 28 and 29 Specimens in folder £32.00			
	1,185 of 7.5k	.925 sterling silver proof		£70.00
	162 of 2.5k	.925 sterling silver Piedfort proof		£120.00
	21 of 750	.917 gold proof, price new (111 also sold in pairs)		£750.00

* Plus another 9,250 pairs of Underground coins combined with stamps.
This Underground Roundal coin has also been seen as an error, completely in brass.

COMMEMORATIVE TYPE 29
Underground Train
1863 | LONDON UNDERGROUND | 2013
(150th anniversary - The London Underground)
Design by: Edward Barber and Jay Osgerby
Edge: A pattern of circles connected by lines.
Obverse: 2b

		Used	BU	Proof
2013	1,690,000	£3.00	£15.00	£15.00
	2,042 of 7.5k	.925 sterling silver proof*		£50.00
	186 of 2.5k	.925 sterling silver Piedfort proof		£120.00
	29 of 750	.917 gold proof, price new (111 also sold in pairs)		£750.00

* A further 2,204 silver proof pairs of both Underground coins were sold : £170

COMMEMORATIVE TYPE 30
Spade Guinea
ANNIVERSARY OF THE GOLDEN GUINEA | 2013
(350th anniversary - the Guinea)
Design by: Anthony Smith
Edge: WHAT IS A GUINEA? 'TIS A SPLENDID THING
Obverse: 2b

		UNC	BU	Proof
2013	2,990,000	£3.00	£16.00	£15.00
	10,340	Specimen in folder	£30.00	
	1640 of 12k	.925 sterling silver proof		£60.00
	969 of 4,013	.925 sterling silver Piedfort proof		£130.00
	284 of 1100	.917 gold proof		£1300.00

28.40 mm • 12.0 grammes • bi-metal • various edge

COMMEMORATIVE TYPE 31
Design from Kitchener recruitment poster
THE FIRST WORLD WAR 1914 - 1918 | 2014
(Centenary - Start of WWI)
Design by: John Bergdahl
Edge: THE LAMPS ARE GOING OUT ALL OVER EUROPE
Obverse: 2b

			UNC	BU	Proof
2014	5,720,000		£3.00	£10.00	£15.00
		Specimen in folder, price new		£20.00	
	8,014 max	.925 sterling silver proof, price new			£50.00
	4,514 max	.925 sterling silver Piedfort proof, price new			£100.00
	825 max	.917 gold proof, price new			£750.00

Errors: One with outer ring made from a 2014 standard 50p. Two seen completely in brass.

COMMEMORATIVE TYPE 32
Top of a Lighthouse
1514 TRINITY HOUSE 2014 | TWO POUNDS
(500 years of Trinity house)
Design by: Joe Whitlock Blundell and David Eccles
Edge: SERVING THE MARINER
Obverse 2

			UNC	BU	Proof
2014	3,705,000		£3.00	£10.00	£15.00
		Specimen in folder, price new		£25.00	
	4,717 max	.925 sterling silver proof, price new			£50.00
	3,514 max	.925 sterling silver Piedfort proof, price new			£100.00
	375 max	.917 gold proof, price new			£750.00

COMMEMORATIVE TYPE 33a
Royal Navy Battleship
THE FIRST WORLD WAR 1914 - 1918 | 2015
(Centenary - WWI, Royal Navy themed coin)
Design by: David Rowlands
Edge: THE SURE SHIELD OF BRITAIN
With Obverse type 2b, shown to right

			BU	Proof
2015		Not circulated, sets / packages only	Proof from set:	£15.00
		Specimen in folder		£16.00
	8,500 max	.925 sterling silver proof, price new		£50.00
	4,000 max	.925 sterling silver Piedfort proof, price new		£100.00
	900 max	.917 gold proof, price new		£750.00

COMMEMORATIVE TYPE 33b
Royal Navy Battleship
THE FIRST WORLD WAR 1914 - 1918 | 2015
(Centenary - WWI, Royal Navy themed coin)
Design by: David Rowlands
Edge: THE SURE SHIELD OF BRITAIN
With Obverse type 3b, shown to right

	Used	BU
2015		
650,000	£5.00	*

* These coins first appeared in circulation in October 2016. The mintage number is low enough to probably lead to people getting excited enough about them and to result in instant higher prices, even though there are plenty to go round. Coins in close to perfect condition will be almost impossible to find due to the recent poor standard of circulation coins.

COMMEMORATIVE TYPE 34a
King John with bishop and a baron
MAGNA CARTA | 1215 - 2015
(King John signing the Magna Carta)
Design by: John Bergdahl
Edge: FOUNDATION OF LIBERTY
With Obverse type 2d, shown to right

		BU	Proof
2015	Not circulated, sets / packages only	Proof from set:	£15.00
	Specimen in folder	£20.00	
1500	.925 sterling silver proof, in sets only*		£75.00?

*This silver proof coin appears to have been made for silver proof sets only, which contain the 5 main commemorative coins of 2015. The main silver proof Magna Carta coins are all Type 34b.

COMMEMORATIVE TYPE 34b
King John with bishop and a baron
MAGNA CARTA | 1215 - 2015
(King John signing the Magna Carta)
Design by: John Bergdahl
Edge: FOUNDATION OF LIBERTY
Obverse type 3d, shown to right

		UNC	BU	Proof
2015	1,495,000	£3.00	*	
	4000 max	.925 sterling silver proof		£55.00
	2000 max	.925 sterling silver piedfort proof		£100.00
	400 max	.917 gold proof, price new		£750.00

* Hard to find in perfect condition due to the poor standard of current circulation coins.

89

The 2015 Commemorative £2 coins on the previous pages lack continuity and can be confusing. For each of the two coins (First World War Navy and Magna Carta) two different obverses were used during the year, one with the 4th portrait of the Queen and the other with the new 5th portrait. There are therefore four basic designs. The whole thing is further complicated by the proof issues, which for the Navy coin all use the 4th portrait and for the Magna Carta coin, use the 5th portrait, except for the base metal proof coin (from sets) which features the 4th portrait and early versions of the Magna Carta silver proof coins which were sold in sets of 2015 commemorative coins and feature the 4th portrait.

COMMEMORATIVE TYPE 35
Stylised representation of 'Pals Battalion'
THE FIRST WORLD WAR 1914 - 1918 | 2016
(Centenary - WWI, Army themed coin)
Design by: Tim Sharp of the creative agency Uniform
Edge: **FOR KING AND COUNTRY**
Obverse 3b

		UNC	BU	Proof
2016		£5.00	£8.00	£12.00
	Specimen in folder, price new		£10.00	
5,000 max	.925 sterling silver proof			£60.00
2,500 max	.925 sterling silver Piedfort proof, price new			£110.00
750 max	.917 gold proof, price new			

COMMEMORATIVE TYPE 36
Scene from the Great Fire of London
1666 THE GREAT FIRE OF LONDON 2016 | TWO POUNDS
(350th Anniversary of the Great Fire of London)
Design by: Aaron West
Edge: **THE WHOLE CITY IN DREADFUL FLAMES**
Obverse 3c

		UNC	BU	Proof
2016	1,170,000 (figure not yet 100% confirmed)	£5.00	£15.00	£16.00
	Specimen in folder, price new		£10.00	
7,500 max	.925 sterling silver proof, price new			£65.00
3,500 max	.925 sterling silver Piedfort proof, price new			£110.00
800 max	.917 gold proof, price new			£825.00*

Types 35 & 36 have been seen in brass without the inner silver coloured part (a mint error). Both were in BU sets.

COMMEMORATIVE TYPE 37
Marotte and Jester's hat
WILLIAM SHAKESPEARE | 2016
(300th Anniversary of Shakespeare's death. Comedy theme)
Design by: John Bergdahl
Edge: **ALL THE WORLDS A STAGE**
Obverse 3b

		BU	Proof
2016	975,000 (figure not yet 100% confirmed) Used: £5.00	£10.00	£19.00
	*The 3 Shakespeare coins in folder, new: £28.00		
5,000 max	.925 sterling silver proof, price new		£65.00
2,500 max	.925 sterling silver Piedfort proof, price new		£110.00
	.917 gold proof, price new		£825.00

COMMEMORATIVE TYPE 38
Crown and Sword
WILLIAM SHAKESPEARE | 2016
(300th Anniversary of Shakespeare's death. History theme)
Design by: John Bergdahl
Edge: **THE HOLLOW CROWN**
Obverse 3b

		BU	Proof
2016	2,405,000 (figure not yet 100% confirmed)	£10.00	£19.00
	*The 3 Shakespeare coins in folder, new: £28.00		
5,000 max	.925 sterling silver proof, price new		£65.00
2,500 max	.925 sterling silver Piedfort proof, price new		£110.00
	.917 gold proof, price new		£825.00

COMMEMORATIVE TYPE 39
Skull and Rose
WILLIAM SHAKESPEARE | 2016
(300th Anniversary of Shakespeare's death. Tragedy theme)
Design by: John Bergdahl
Edge: **WHAT A PIECE OF WORK IS A MAN**
Obverse 3b

		BU	Proof
2016	1,560,000 (figure not yet 100% confirmed)	£10.00	£19.00
	*The 3 Shakespeare coins in folder, new: £28.00		
5,000 max	.925 sterling silver proof, price new		£65.00
2,500 max	.925 sterling silver Piedfort proof, price new		£110.00
300 max	.917 gold proof, price new		£825.00

* These 3 coins in Brilliant Uncirculated form were only released together.

91

COMMEMORATIVE TYPE 40
Jane Austen Silhouette and signature
JANE AUSTEN 1817 - 2017 | TWO POUNDS
(200th Anniversary of Jane Austen's death)
Design by: Dominique Evans
Edge: **THERE IS NO DOING WITHOUT MONEY**
Obverse 3

		BU	Proof
2017	Currently in sets only	£15.00	£15.00
	.925 sterling silver proof, price new:		TBC
	.925 sterling silver Piedfort proof, price new		TBC
	.917 gold proof, price new		TBC

COMMEMORATIVE TYPE 41
Biplane from above
1914 - 1918 | THE WAR IN THE AIR
(Centenary - WWI, Aviation themed coin)
Design by: tangerine (design agency)
Edge: **THE SKY RAINED HEROES**
Obverse 3e

		BU	Proof
2017	Currently in sets only	£15.00	£15.00
	.925 sterling silver proof, price new:		TBC
	.925 sterling silver Piedfort proof, price new		TBC
	.917 gold proof, price new		TBC

What's currently legal tender?

All £5 coins are legal tender. Look out for non UK £5 coins being offered for face value as these are often from smaller provinces/islands and are therefore not legal tender in the United Kingdom (and often aren't legal tender in the province stated on them either). Particularly worrying are the coins from Tristan da Cunha, a tiny island group with a population of less than 300. So-called £5 coins from Tristan da Cunha often look very British but simply have 'TDC' in the legend. Also, earlier crown coins should not be confused with these post-1990 £5 crowns. The crowns struck from 1972 to 1981 have a face value of 25p.

Which are hard to find?

All of these large coins are hard to find in circulation because they tend to get hoarded by the public when they are new and they are also made in lower numbers than the lower denominations. They are also heavy and not really practical to carry around for day-to-day transactions. The COMMEMORATIVE TYPE 7 with the 2000 date on the obverse seems scarcer than the 1999 dated millennium coin.

COMMEMORATIVE TYPE 1
Standard portrait of QE II
Design by: Raphael Maklouf
Double "E" monogram, crowned
Design by: Leslie Durbin

			UNC	BU	Proof
1990	2,761,431		£6.00	£7.00	£10.00
	Specimen in card/folder			£10.00	
	56,102	.925 sterling silver proof			£25.00
	2,750	.917 gold proof			£1700.00

COMMEMORATIVE TYPE 2
Mary Gillick portrait of QEII
design by: Robert Elderton
St. Edward's crown
Design by: Robert Elderton

			UNC	BU	Proof
1993	1,834,655		£6.00	£7.00	£10.00
	Specimen in folder			£9.00	
	75,000	.925 sterling silver proof			£25.00
	2,750	.917 gold proof			£1900.00

COMMEMORATIVE TYPE 3
Standard portrait of QE II
Design by: Raphael Maklouf
Windsor Castle and Pennants
Design by: Avril Vaughan
Edge:
VIVAT REGINA ELIZABETHA

			UNC	BU	Proof
1996	2,396,100		£6.00	£7.00	£10.00
		Specimen in folder		£9.00	
	75,000	.925 sterling silver proof			£25.00
	2,750	.917 gold proof			£1700.00

COMMEMORATIVE TYPE 4
Conjoined busts of Elizabeth II
and Prince Philip
Design by: Philip Nathan
Arms of the Royal Couple,
crown, anchor. Design by: Leslie
Durbin

			UNC	BU	Proof
1997	1,733,000		£6.00	£7.00	£10.00
		Specimen in folder		£9.00	
	33,689	.925 sterling silver proof			£25.00
	2,750	.917 gold proof			£1700.00

COMMEMORATIVE TYPE 5
Standard portrait of QE II
Design by: Ian Rank-Broadley
Prince Charles, "The Prince's Trust"
Design by: Michael Noakes

			UNC	BU	Proof
1998	1,407,300	100,000	£5.50	£7.00	£10.00
		Specimen in folder		£9.00	
	35,000	.925 sterling silver proof			£25.00
	2,000	.917 gold proof			£1700.00

COMMEMORATIVE TYPE 6
Standard portrait of QEII
Design by: Ian Rank-Broadley
Portrait of Princess Diana
Design by: David Cornell

		UNC	BU	Proof
1999	5,396,300 (for both 1999 crowns)	£5.50	£7.00	£10.00
	Specimen in folder		£9.00	
49,545	.925 sterling silver proof			£25.00
2,750	.917 gold proof			£1700.00

COMMEMORATIVE TYPE 7
Standard portrait of QE II
(Dated either 1999 or 2000)
Design by: Ian Rank-Broadley
Clock at midnight, with map
of British Isles
Design by: Jeffrey Matthews
Edge:
WHAT'S PAST IS PROLOGUE

		UNC	BU	Proof
Dated 1999 on Obverse	5,396,300 (inc. Type 6)	£5.50	£7.00	£10.00
	Specimen in folder		£9.00	
75,000	.925 sterling silver cased proof			£25.00
2,750	.917 gold cased proof			£1700.00
Dated 2000 on Obverse (not shown)		£10.00	£15.00	£15.00
3,147,092*	Specimen in folder		£15.00	
75,000	.925 sterling silver proof			£40.00
2,750	.917 gold proof			£2,000.00

COMMEMORATIVE TYPE 7a (SEE NEXT PAGE)

As above, with special dome mint-mark, available only at the **Millennium Dome.**
2000	Specimen in folder	£20.00

* Mintage is combined total for this coin and Type 8. Individual totals are not know.

TYPE 7a: Picture showing the location of the dome mint-mark, to the upper right of 'ANNO DOMINI'.

COMMEMORATIVE TYPE 8
Standard portrait of QE II
Design by: Ian Rank-Broadley
Portrait of the Queen Mother
Design by: Ian Rank-Broadley

			UNC	BU	Proof
2000	3,147,092 (for both Type 8 and Type 7)		£5.50	£7.00	£10.00
		Specimen in folder		£9.00	
	100,000	.925 sterling silver proof			£30.00
	14,850	.925 sterling silver Piedfort proof			£35.00
	2,750	.917 gold proof			£1700.00

COMMEMORATIVE TYPE 9
Standard portrait of QEII
Design by: Ian Rank-Broadley
Wyon portrait of Victoria
Design by: Mary Milner Dickens

			UNC	BU	Proof
2001	851,491		£6.00	£8.00	£10.00
	44,090	Specimen in folder		£11.00	
	19,812	.925 sterling silver proof			£30.00
	2,831	.917 gold proof			£1700.00

COMMEMORATIVE TYPE 10
Queen Elizabeth II on horseback
Design by: Ian Rank-Broadley
Queen wearing robes and diadem
Design by: Ian Rank-Broadley

		UNC	BU	Proof
2002		£5.50	£7.00	£10.00
340,230	Specimen in folder		£9.00	
54,012	.925 sterling silver proof			£30.00
3,461	.917 gold proof			£1700.00

COMMEMORATIVE TYPE 11
Standard portrait of QEII
Design by: Ian Rank-Broadley
Portrait of Queen Mother
Design by: Avril Vaughan.
Edge: STRENGTH DIGNITY LAUGHTER

		UNC	BU	Proof
2002		£5.50	£7.00	£10.00
	Specimen in folder		£9.00	
35,000	.925 sterling silver proof			£30.00
2,750	.917 gold proof			£1700.00

COMMEMORATIVE TYPE 12
Sketched portrait of QE II
Design by: Tom Philips
"GOD SAVE THE QUEEN"
Design by: Tom Philips

		UNC	BU	Proof
2003	1,307,010	£5.50	£7.00	£10.00
	Specimen in folder		£9.00	
75,000	.925 sterling silver proof			£30.00
3,500	.917 gold proof			£1700.00

97

COMMEMORATIVE TYPE 13
Standard portrait of QEII
Design by: Ian Rank-Broadley
Conjoined Britannia and Marianne
Design by: David Gentlemen

			UNC	BU	Proof
2004	1,205,594	(+ 16,507 in folders)	£6.00	£8.00	£10.00*
	11,295 of 15k	.925 sterling silver proof			£30.00
	2,500	.925 sterling silver piedfort proof			£60.00
	926 of 1,500	.917 gold proof			£1700.00
	501	.9995 platinum cased proof (3.0271 troy oz)			£3,800.00

* Was also sold as a cased base metal proof with certificate, value £20 - £25.

COMMEMORATIVE TYPE 14
Standard portrait of QE II
design by: Ian Rank-Broadley
Portrait of Horatio Nelson
design by: James Butler
Edge: ENGLAND EXPECTS EVERYMAN TO DO HIS DUTY

			UNC	BU	Proof
2005	1,075,516 inc. Type 15		£5.50	£7.00	£10.00
	72,498	Specimen in folder		£11.00	
	12,852	.925 sterling silver proof			£30.00
	1,760	.917 gold proof			£1700.00

COMMEMORATIVE TYPE 15
Standard portrait of QEII
design by: Ian Rank-Broadley
HMS Victory & Temeraire
design by: Clive Duncan

			UNC	BU	Proof
2005	Inc. above, with Type 14		£5.50	£7.00	£10.00
	79,868	Specimen in folder		£11.00	
	Specimen set (contains both 2005 folders, in sleeve)		£25.00		
	21,448	.925 sterling silver proof			£30.00
	1,805	.917 gold proof			£1700.00

COMMEMORATIVE TYPE 16
Standard portrait of QEII
Design by: Ian Rank-Broadley
Ceremonial Trumpets
with Banners
Design by:
Danuta Solowiej-Wedderburn
Edge: DUTY SERVICE FAITH

			UNC	BU	Proof
2006			£5.50	£7.00	£10.00
	330,790	Specimen in folder		£9.00	
	20,790 of 50k	.925 sterling silver proof			£30.00
	5,000	.925 sterling silver piedfort proof			£80.00
	2,750	.917 gold proof			£1700.00

COMMEMORATIVE TYPE 17
Standard portrait of QEII
Design by: Ian Rank-Broadley
The North Rose Window at
Westminster Abbey
Design by: Emma Noble
Edge: MY STRENGTH AND STAY

			UNC	BU	Proof
2007	2,396,100		£5.50	£7.00	£10.00
	260,856	Specimen in folder		£10.00	
	15,186 of 35k	.925 sterling silver proof			£40.00
	2,000 of 5,000	.925 sterling silver piedfort proof			£80.00
	2,380 of 2,500	.917 gold proof			£1700.00
	250	Platinum piedfort proof			£4000.00

COMMEMORATIVE TYPE 18
Standard portrait of QEII
Design by: Ian Rank-Broadley
Portrait of Elizabeth I
Westminster Abbey
Design by: Rod Kelly
Edge: (proofs only)I HAVE
REIGNED WITH YOUR LOVES

		UNC	BU	Proof
2008	30,649	£5.50	£7.00	£18.00
	Specimen in folder		£10.00	
9,216 of 20k	.925 sterling silver proof			£40.00
1,602 of 2k	.925 sterling silver piedfort proof			£70.00
1,500	.917 gold proof			£1700.00
125 of 150	Platinum piedfort proof			£4000.00

COMMEMORATIVE TYPE 19
Standard portrait of QEII
Design by: Ian Rank-Broadley
Portrait of the Price of Wales
Design by: Ian Rank-Broadley
Edge: SIXTIETH BIRTHDAY

		UNC	BU	Proof
2008	54,746	£5.50	£7.00	£18.00
	Specimen in folder		£10.00	
6,264	.925 sterling silver proof			£35.00
1088 of 5k	.925 sterling silver piedfort proof			£80.00
867 of 1500	.917 gold proof			£1700.00
54 of 150	Platinum piedfort proof			£4000.00

COMMEMORATIVE TYPE 20
Standard portrait of QEII
Design by: Ian Rank-Broadley
Henry VIII
Design by: John Bergdahl

			UNC	BU	Proof
2009	67,119		£5.50	£7.00	£25.00
		Specimen in folder		£20.00	
	10,419 of 20k	.925 sterling silver proof			£35.00
	3,580 of 4009	.925 sterling silver piedfort proof			£100.00
	1130 of 1509	.917 gold proof			£1700.00
	100	Platinum piedfort proof			£4000.00

COMMEMORATIVE TYPE 21
Standard portrait of QEII
Design by: Ian Rank-Broadley
Countdown '3'
Design by: Claire Aldridge

			UNC	BU	Proof
2009	184,921		£5.50	£7.00	£10.00
		Specimen in folder		£10.00	
	26,645 of 30k	.925 sterling silver proof			£40.00
	4,874 of 6k	.925 sterling silver piedfort proof			£80.00
	1860 of 4000	.917 gold proof			£1700.00

Celebration of Britain: Mind, Body and Spirit 2009 - 2010.

CAUTION: Chinese made forgeries of this series exist. The fakes have inconsistently frosted details and poorly executed colouring of the '2012' logos.

The Royal Mint issued a whopping eighteen different crowns in conjunction with the London 2012 Olympics, eleven of which are shown on the following pages. Starting in June 2009, one was issued every twenty-eight days until late 2010. The eighteen coins were made available as a complete set (one of which, with original packaging, box etc sold for nearly £900.00) as well as being available in groups of six (themed: 'Mind', 'Body' and 'Spirit').

They were all struck as sterling silver proofs. Three of them: the Clock-face (1), London (15) and Churchill (16) coins were also struck in cupro-nickel. The obverse design is the same as that used for COMMEMORATIVE TYPE 24, but dated either 2009 or 2010, as indicated. The reverse designs are all of a high standard and by Shane Greeves. Each design is accompanied by some wise words with a very loose connections to the subject matter of the designs featured.

CELEBRATION TYPE 1
Mind Series (with green London 2012 logo)
Clock-face of the Palace of Westminster
Walter Bagehot quote:
"Nations touch at their summits"

2009	.925 Sterling silver proof (95k max.)	£30-£40
2009	Cupro-Nickel proof (100k max.)	£20-£25

CELEBRATION TYPE 2
Mind Series (with green London 2012 logo)
Stonehenge
William Blake quote:
"Great things are done when men and mountains meet"

2009	.925 Sterling silver proof (95k max.)	£30-£40

CELEBRATION TYPE 2
Mind Series (with green London 2012 logo)
The Angel of the North
William Shakespeare quote:
"I have touched the highest point of all my greatness"

2009	.925 Sterling silver proof (95k max.)	£30-£40

CELEBRATION TYPE 4
Mind Series (with green London 2012 logo)
The Flying Scotsman
William Shakespeare quote:
"True hope is swift"

2009   .925 Sterling silver proof (95k max.)   £30-£40

CELEBRATION TYPE 5
Mind Series (with green London 2012 logo)
Sculpture of Isaac Newton
William Shakespeare quote:
"Make not your thoughts your prisons"

2009   .925 Sterling silver proof (95k max.)   £30-£40

CELEBRATION TYPE 6
Mind Series (with green London 2012 logo)
The Globe Theatre
William Shakespeare quote:
"We are such stuff as dreams are made of"

2009   .925 Sterling silver proof (95k max.)   £30-£40

CELEBRATION TYPE 7
Body Series (with red London 2012 logo)
Rhossili Bay
William Blake quote:
"To see a world in a grain of sand"

2010   .925 Sterling silver proof (95k max.)   £30-£40

CELEBRATION TYPE 8
Body Series (with red London 2012 logo)
Giant's Causeway
Alice Oswald quote:
"When the stone began to dream"

2010   .925 Sterling silver proof (95k max.)   £30-£40

Celebration of Britain: Mind, Body and Spirit 2009 - 2010 (continued).

CELEBRATION TYPE 9
Body Series (with red London 2012 logo)
The River Thames
Percy Bysshe Shelley quote:
"Tameless, and swift, and proud"

2010   .925 Sterling silver proof (95k max.)   £30-£40

CELEBRATION TYPE 10
Body Series (with red London 2012 logo)
Barn Owl
Samuel Johnson quote:
"The natural flights of the human mind"

2010   .925 Sterling silver proof (95k max.)   £30-£40

CELEBRATION TYPE 11
Body Series (with red London 2012 logo)
Oak leaves and an acorn
Alfred, Lord Tennyson quote:
"To strive, to seek ... and not to yield"

2010   .925 Sterling silver proof (95k max.)   £30-£40

CELEBRATION TYPE 12
Body Series (with red London 2012 logo)
Weather-vane
Charlotte Brontë quote:
"Never may a cloud come o'er the sunshine of your mind"

2010   .925 Sterling silver proof (95k max.)   £30-£40

CELEBRATION TYPE 13
Spirit Series (with blue London 2012 logo)
Floral emblems of the UK
John Lennon quote:
"And the world will be as one"

2010   .925 Sterling silver proof (95k max.)   £30-£40

CELEBRATION TYPE 14
Spirit Series (with blue London 2012 logo)
White rabbit from Alice in Wonderland
T S Elliot quote:
"All touched by a common genius"

2010 .925 Sterling silver proof (95k max.) £30-£40

CELEBRATION TYPE 15
Spirit Series (with blue London 2012 logo)
View down the Mall, London
Alfred, Lord Tennyson quote:
"Kind hearts are more than coronets"

2010 .925 Sterling silver proof (95k max.) £30-£40
2010 Cupro-Nickel proof (100k max.) £20-£25

CELEBRATION TYPE 16
Spirit Series (with blue London 2012 logo)
Winston Churchill Statue
Anita Roddick quote:
"Be daring, be first, be different, be just"

2010 .925 Sterling silver proof (95k max.) £30-£40
2010 Cupro-Nickel proof (100k max.) £20-£25

CELEBRATION TYPE 17
Spirit Series (with blue London 2012 logo)
Musical instruments sculpture
Lennon & McCartney quote:
"All you need is love"

2010 .925 Sterling silver proof (95k max.) £30-£40

CELEBRATION TYPE 18
Spirit Series (with blue London 2012 logo)
Image of campaigner Equiano
William Shakespeare quote:
"To thine own self be true"

2010 .925 Sterling silver proof (95k max.) £30-£40

COMMEMORATIVE TYPE 22
Standard portrait of QEII
Design by: Ian Rank-Broadley
1660 Restoration of Monarchy
Design by: David Cornell
Obverse: Type as no. 20

		UNC	BU	Proof
2010	(all originally sold in folders/proof sets)	£5.50	£7.00	£10.00
30,247	Specimen in folder		£10.00	
6,518 of 20k	.925 sterling silver proof			£40.00
4,435 of 5k	.925 sterling silver piedfort proof			£70.00
1,182 of 1,200	.917 gold proof			£1700.00
100 max	Platinum piedfort proof			£?

COMMEMORATIVE TYPE 23
Standard portrait of QEII
Design by: Ian Rank-Broadley
Countdown '2'
Design by: Claire Aldridge

		UNC	BU	Proof
2010	(all originally sold in folders)	£5.50	£7.00	
153,080	Specimen in folder		£10.00	
20,159 of 30k	.925 sterling silver proof			£40.00
4,435	.925 sterling silver piedfort proof			£80.00
1,562 of 3k	.917 gold proof			£1700.00

As part of the Royal Mints unprecedented drive to make as many themed coins as possible, since becoming Royal Mint Ltd in 2010, higher face value coins were also issued. In silver: a £10 with a diameter of 65mm and weight of 5oz (155.5g) featuring the winged horse pegasus. A £500 with a diameter of 100mm and weight of one kilogram, featuring the stylised words 'XXX OLYMPIAD'.

Gold olympic themed coins consisted of 6x £25 coins (2 each for 'faster', 'higher' and 'stronger'), 3x £100 coins (one each for 'faster', 'higher' and 'stronger') and a crude looking one kilogram gold coin with a face value of £1000.

COMMEMORATIVE TYPE 24
Standard portrait of QEII
Design by: Ian Rank-Broadley
**Royal Wedding of William &
Catherine**
Design by: Mark Richards

		UNC	BU	Proof
2011	(all originally sold in folders)	£7.00	£9.00	
250,000	Specimen in folder		£20.00	
26,069 of 50k	.925 sterling silver proof/or 7,451 max gold plated coin*£40.00			
2,991 of 3k	.925 sterling silver piedfort proof			£80.00
2,066 of 3k	.917 gold proof			£1700.00
133 of 200	Platinum piedfort proof			£4000.00

*The previous gold plated maximum mintage of 3,000 seems to have been raised.

COMMEMORATIVE TYPE 25
Standard portrait of QEII
Design by: Ian Rank-Broadley
Countdown '1'
Design by: Claire Aldridge

		UNC	BU	Proof
2011	(all originally sold in folders)	£6.00	£7.00	£10.00
163,235	Specimen in folder		£10.00	
25,877 of 30k	.925 sterling silver proof			£40.00
4000	.925 sterling silver piedfort proof			£80.00
1,300 of 3k	.917 gold proof			£1700.00

COMMEMORATIVE TYPE 26
Standard portrait of QEII
Design by: Ian Rank-Broadley
Prince Philip 90th Birthday
Design by: Mark Richards

		UNC	BU	Proof
2011	(all originally sold in folders/proof sets)	£20.00	£30.00	£30.00
18,730	Specimen in folder		£35.00	
4,599 of 20k	.925 sterling silver proof			£60.00
2,659 of 4k	.925 sterling silver piedfort proof			£80.00
636 of 1,200	.917 gold proof			£1700.00
49 of 90	Platinum piedfort proof			£4000.00

COMMEMORATIVE TYPE 27
Standard portrait of QEII
Design by: Ian Rank-Broadley
Countdown '0'
Design by: Claire Aldridge

		UNC	BU	Proof
2012	(all originally sold in folders)	£5.50	£7.00	
52,261*	Specimen in folder/card		£10.00	
12,670 of 30k	.925 sterling silver proof			£40.00
2,324 of 4k	.925 sterling silver piedfort proof			£80.00
1,007 of 3k	.917 gold proof			£2000.00

* Plus 13,014 in packaging combining stamps with the coin.

COMMEMORATIVE TYPE 28
Standard portrait of QEII
Design by: Ian Rank-Broadley
London 2012 Olympics
Commemorative
Design by: Siaman Miah
Obverse: Type as no. 24

		UNC	BU	Proof
2012	(all originally sold in folders)		£8.00	
315,983*	Specimen in folder		£10.00	
20,810 of 100k	.925 sterling silver proof			£30.00
5,946 of 7k	.925 sterling silver piedfort proof			£100.00
8,180 of 12.5k	.925 sterling silver, gold plating*			£80.00
1,045 of 5k	.917 gold proof			£2000.00

* Plus 13,959 in packaging combining stamps with the coin.

20x 2012 £1000 face value gold Olympic games coins were sold. Other proof gold coins included six classical Olympics themed £25 coins and three £100 coins. Full sets are still available new for £10,500. 5,056 5oz silver coins were sold and 910x £500FV 1kg coins were sold.

COMMEMORATIVE TYPE 29
Standard portrait of QEII
Design by: Ian Rank-Broadley
London 2012 Paralympics
Commemorative
Design by: Pippa Sanderson
Obverse: Type as no. 24

		UNC	BU	Proof
2012	(all originally sold in folders)		£10.00	
52,261*	Specimen in folder		£30.00	
10,000/3,000*	.925 sterling silver proof / or gold plated version			£40.00
2012 max	.925 sterling silver piedfort proof			£100.00
5000 max	.917 gold proof			£2000.00

* Plus 13,014 in packaging combining stamps with the coin.

COMMEMORATIVE TYPE 30
Special portrait of QEII
Design by: Ian Rank-Broadley
Queen's Diamond Jubilee
Design by: Ian Rank-Broadley

		BU	Proof
2012		£7.00	
	[961 base metal proofs sold separately]		£10.00
484,775*	Specimen in folder	£10.00	
16,820 of 75k	.925 sterling silver proof		£40.00
3,187 of 3,250	.925 sterling silver piedfort proof		£100.00
12,112 of 12.5k	.925 sterling silver, gold plated*		?
1,085 of 3,850	.917 gold proof		£2200.00
20 of 250	Platinum piedfort proof		£5000.00

To mark the Jubilee there was also a £10 coin (as silver or gold proof) with a diameter of 65mm -
these have the same obverse as above and feature the queen enthroned and facing on the reverse.
Prices new were about £450 for the silver version (1933 sold) and £9,500 for the gold coin (they
sold 140). One kilogram silver (£500FV, 206 sold) and one kilogram gold (£1000FV, 21 sold) coins
were also made to mark the Queens jubilee. Both use the same obverse as above and show the full
Royal Arms on the reverse.

* Plus 18,948 in packages combining stamps with the coin.

COMMEMORATIVE TYPE 31
Standard portrait of QEII
Design by: Ian Rank-Broadley
Anniversary of Coronation
Design by: Emma Noble
Obverse: Type as no. 24

		UNC	BU	Proof
2013	(all originally sold in folders / proof sets)	£5.50	£7.00	£10.00
57,262*	Specimen in folder		£10.00	
6,667 of 15k	.925 sterling silver proof			£70.00
3,185 of 3,250	.925 sterling silver piedfort proof, price new			£160.00
2,547 of 12.5k	.925 sterling silver, gold plated			?
458 of 2,000	.917 gold proof, price new			£1800.00
106 of 100 max!	Platinum piedfort proof, price new			£6400.00

*Plus 11,642 in packages combining stamps with the coin.
301x £500 1kg silver proofs were sold. 1604 x 5oz silver proofs were also sold.

COMMEMORATIVE TYPES 32a & 32b
Standard portrait of QEII
Design by: Ian Rank-Broadley
32a: Birth of Prince George
32b: Christening of Prince George
Design by: Benedetto Pistrucci (Birth). John Bergdahl (Christening)
Obverses: Both as Type no. 23

32a

32b

			UNC	BU	Proof
2013	7,460*	(32a) .925 sterling silver proof only			£250.00
		(32b)		£10.00	£14.00
	56,014	(32b) Specimen in folder		£16.00	
	7,264 of 75k	(32b) .925 sterling silver proof			£50.00
	2,251 of 2.5k	(32b) .925 sterling silver piedfort proof			£180.00
	486 of 1000	(32b) .917 gold proof			£2000.00
	38 of 100	(32b) Platinum piedfort proof			?

*Shortly after the birth of Prince George, a silver proof only £5 Crown was released with the Pistrucci St. George Reverse. This was the first coin that the Royal Mint refused to sell to other businesses, offering it exclusively to their private customers for £80. Apparently 25 platinum proof versions of the birth coin were also made.

Note that for both the 2013 coronation (no. 31) and Prince George (no.32b) one kilo versions with a face value of £500 were struck in silver. These were both available new for £2600. Gold kilo versions of no. 32b were also sold.

THE QUEEN'S PORTRAIT SET (2013)

Reverse   Gillick Obverse   Machin Obverse

Coins featuring the four Portraits of the Queen used on coinage -
Three previous obverses and the current obverse of the time,
by: Mary Gillick, Arnold Machin, Raphael Maklouf and Ian Rank-Broadley
Reverse Design (common to all), the Royal Arms by: James Butler

This set of four coins produced in 2013, available only in sets struck in either .925 silver or .917 gold. All four coins share the same reverse. The obverses used are as follows:
Coin 1: A re-worked Mary Gillick obverse with 'FIVE POUNDS' under the bust.
Coin 2: A re-worked Arnold Machin obverse with new legend to incorporate 'FIVE POUNDS'.
Coin 3: Appears to be the same reverse as used on the 1990 Crown (Commemorative Type 1).
Coin 4: One of the standard obverses of the time that first appeared on the 2002 Crown (Commemorative Type 11) and is also shown on the following page for Commemorative Type 34.

Proof

2013	1,465 of 4,800 max	.925 silver proof set of 4, price new	£400.00
	150 of 450	.917 gold proof set of 4, price new	£7,200.00

COMMEMORATIVE TYPE 33
Standard portrait of QEII
Design by: Ian Rank-Broadley
300th Anniversary of the Death of Queen Anne
Design by: Mark Richards
Obverse: Type as no. 24

		UNC	BU	Proof
2014	(all originally sold in folders/proof sets)	£10.00		£23.00
	Specimen in folder		£13.00	
	3100 max	.925 sterling silver proof			£40.00
	1665 max	.925 sterling silver, gold plated			£60.00
(was 2014 max)	4028 max	.925 sterling silver piedfort proof			£85.00
	375 max	.917 gold proof, price new			£1800.00
	250 max?	Platinum piedfort proof			?

COMMEMORATIVE TYPE 34
Standard portrait of QEII
Design by: Ian Rank-Broadley
Re-used 1953/1960 reverse to
mark the 1st birthday
of Prince George
Design by:
Edgar Fuller & Cecil Thomas
Edge: Milled

			Proof
2014			
	7,500 max	.925 sterling silver proof only	£80.00

Ten further Crowns struck in 2014!
A Portrait of Britain Set of Four Crowns and the first set of six for WWI:
In 2014 a set of four .925 sterling silver proof coins dubbed 'The Portrait of Britain Collection' was sold new for £360.00. The reverses by Glyn Davies and Laura Clancy featured Tri-Chromatic pad printed images of The Elizabeth Tower (Big Ben), Buckingham Palace, Tower Bridge and Trafalgar Square. Maximum mintage was 3,500.

And if that wasn't enough, the first set of six .925 sterling silver proof only coins were produced to mark WWI, using the same obverse type as COMMEMORATIVE TYPE 24 . This set was £450.00 new and a maximum of 1914 complete sets were produced. Sorry, no pictures yet!

COMMEMORATIVE TYPE 35
Standard portrait of QEII
Design by: Ian Rank-Broadley
Winston Churchill - 50th Anniversary of his death
Design by: Mark Richards
Obverse: Type as no. 24
Edge (on proofs): NEVER FLINCH, NEVER WEARY,
NEVER DESPAIR

		UNC	BU	Proof
2015		£7.00	£8.00	£15.00
	Specimen in folder		£10.00	
7,500 max	.925 sterling silver proof			£75.00
2,000 max	.925 sterling silver piedfort proof, price new			£160.00
?	.925 sterling silver, gold plated			?
620 max	.917 gold proof, price new			£1800.00
65 max	Platinum piedfort proof, price new			£5000.00

COMMEMORATIVE TYPE 36a and 36b
Standard portrait of QEII
Design by: Ian Rank-Broadley (36a) or Jody Clark (36b)
Battle of Waterloo - 200th Anniversary
Design by: David Lawrence
Obverse: Type as no. 24 (for 36a) or as no. 41 (for 36b)
Edge (on proofs): THE NEAREST RUN THING YOU EVER SAW

			UNC	BU	Proof
2015		(36a)	£8.00	£10.00	£12.00
		(36a) Specimen in folder		£16.00	
	3,000 max	(36b)* .925 sterling silver proof, price new			£80.00
	1500 max	(36a) .925 sterling silver proof, part of set of 5 coins			£100.00?
	1500 max	(36b) .925 sterling silver piedfort proof, price new			£160.00
	500 max	(36b) .917 gold proof, price new			£1945.00

*The main individually boxed silver proof coins of this type feature the 5th portrait, Some were also made as silver proof with the 4th portrait, available only in sets of 5x 2015 silver proof coins.

COMMEMORATIVE TYPE 37
Standard portrait of QEII
Design by: Jody Clark
Birth of Princess Charlotte
Design by: John Bergdahl
Edge: Milled (non proof)

		UNC	BU	Proof
2015		£8.00	£10.00	£22.00
	Specimen in folder		£14.00	
4,500 max	.925 sterling silver proof			£35.00
250 max	.917 gold proof, price new			£1800.00

See also COMMEMORATIVE TYPE 39 for the Princess Charlotte Christening coin.

FIRST WORLD WAR, 2015 SIX COIN SET

Albert Ball VC	Animals at war	Submarines
Edith Cavell	Merchant Navy	Gallipoli

The second set of six coins produced to mark WWI, struck in .925 silver. All six coins share the same obverse (the same used on Commemorative Type 4). The reverses used are as follows:

Coin 1: Albert Ball VC, by David Cornell. Edge: BY FAR THE BEST ENGLISH FLYING MAN.
Coin 2: Animals at war, by David Lawrence. Edge: PATIENT EYES COURAGEOUS HEARTS.
Coin 3: Submarines, by Edwina Ellis. Edge: IN LITTLE BOXES MADE OF TIN.
Coin 4: Edith Cavell, by David Cornell. Edge: SHE FACED THEM GENTLE AND BOLD.
Coin 5: Merchant Navy, by David Rowlands. Edge: SEPULCHRED IN THE HARBOUR OF THE DEEP.
Coin 6: Gallipoli, by John Bergdahl. Edge: HEROES THAT SHED THEIR BLOOD.

Proof

2015   1,915 max   .925 silver proof set of 6, price new   £465.00

Maximum mintage for each coin was marked as 2,500 with the exception of the Gallipoli coin, which was 5,000. This would imply that the coins also appear singly and not just in sets of six. They don't seem to have been very popular though, as they are still available at the end of 2016 and the Royal Mint offered them at a discount through their eBay account - I was able to purchase a set for about £260.00, hence the more extensive coverage and my own photographs on this page!

COMMEMORATIVE TYPE 38
Alternative portrait of QEII
Design by: James Butler
Longest Reigning Monarch
Design by: James Butler
Edge (on precious metal proofs):
LONG TO REIGN OVER US

			UNC	BU	Proof
2015	(all originally sold in folders)		£8.00	£9.00	
		Specimen in folder		£10.00	
	9,000 max	.925 sterling silver proof			£80.00
	3,700 max	.925 sterling silver piedfort proof, price new			£160.00
	1650 max	.917 gold proof, price new			£1650.00
	63 max	.Platinum proof, price new			£5000.00

See also the Longest Reigning Monarch £20 coin, the design of which was also used on larger size silver and gold proof coins, which were very expensive new and are rarely offered.

COMMEMORATIVE TYPE 39
Standard Fifth portrait of QEII
Design by: Jody Clark
Christening of
Princess Charlotte
Design by: John Bergdahl
Edge: Milled

		Proof
2015		
	4,500 max	.925 sterling silver proof only, price new	£80.00

COMMEMORATIVE TYPE 40
Standard Fifth portrait of QEII
Design by: Jody Clark
Second Birthday of Prince George
Design by: Christopher Le Brun
Obverse: Same as TYPE 39
Edge: Milled

			Proof
2015			
	7,500 max	.925 sterling silver proof only, price new	£80.00

COMMEMORATIVE TYPE 41
Standard Fifth portrait of QEII
Design by: Jody Clark
Queen's 90th Birthday
Design by: Christopher Hobbs
Edge (on precious metal proofs):
FULL OF HONOUR AND YEARS

			BU	Proof
2016	(all originally sold in folders/proof sets)		£15.00	£20.00
	13,000 max	.925 sterling silver proof, price new		£80.00
	7,000 max	.925 sterling silver piedfort proof, price new		£155.00
	1200 max	.917 gold proof, price new		£1700.00
	90 max	Platinum piedfort proof, price new		£A lot!

This coin design was also used for 5oz silver, gold and 1kg silver coins. They are rarely offered.

Another Portrait of Britain Set of Four Crowns: In 2016 a second (the first set was sold in 2014) set of four .925 sterling silver proof coins dubbed 'Portrait of Britain 2016 UK £5 Silver Collection' was sold new for £295.00. The reverses by Glyn Davies and Laura Clancy feature Tri-Chromatic pad printed images of The White Cliffs of Dover, Giants Causeway, Lake District and Snowdonia. Maximum mintage is 2,016. Interesting to note the reductions in both price and mintage over the 2014 set. Sorry, no pictures yet!

FIRST WORLD WAR, 2016 SIX COIN SET

And another set of six coins produced in 2016, the third set to mark WWI, struck in .925 silver. All six coins share the same obverse (the same used on Commemorative Type 41.) Information about the reverses used was not available at time of writing. One of the coins is currently available separately and is shown on the next page as Commemorative Type 'Somme'.

			Proof
2015	1,916 max	.925 silver proof set of 6, price new	£465.00

Maximum mintage for each coin was not available.

My opinion: The Royal Mint have produced rather a lot of silver-proof-only £5 coins over the last few years. They are a business (at least, the commemorative coins side of things is a business) and their imperative is to make as much profit as possible. Clearly they make more profit selling silver proof £5 crown coins for around £75 - £80 each, than they do producing larger numbers of base metal £5 crown coins and selling them for around £13 in card packaging.

Gone are the days where you used to be able to buy a bog-standard £5 crown coin for £5*. To me, if a coin never circulates, isn't actually meant to circulate and doesn't even exist in a standard circulation form (not even in base metal form) and the only way you can get one is by buying it new, then it's not a coin at all in the strictest sense, it's simply a medal with a denomination marked on it. The Royal Mint have a huge advantage in that they can create as many products as they like and basically have the exclusive right to mark any denomination on them that they care to.

The public no longer have the pleasure of discovering new crowns in change or at their local Post Office/bank and if people did want to own them all, they'd have to shell out £760 for 10 silver-proof-only £5 coins just for 2016 alone. I feel that is financially out of reach for most. In future editions I will re-organise things and banish these silver-proof-only sets to the back of the Five Pounds section!

* Not to be confused with the other offers from different companies of £5 coins for £5, which are nearly always coins marked as £5 made for tiny islands and territories, rather than proper legal tender UK coinage and/or are simply ploys to get you on a mailing list.

COMMEMORATIVE TYPE SOMME
Standard Fifth portrait of QEII
Design by: Jody Clark
Battle of the Somme, 100th Anniversary.
Design by: John Bergdahl
Edge:
DEAD MEN CAN ADVANCE NO FURTHER
Obverse: As Type 41.

			Proof
2016			
	6,000* max	.925 sterling silver proof only, price new	£82.50

*Apparently the boxed proof coins are limited to 1,916. The total maximum mintage is 6,000. I'm not sure how the others will be sold.

COMMEMORATIVE TYPE 42
Standard Fifth portrait of QEII
Design by: Jody Clark
King Canute
Design by: Lee R. Jones
Edge: Milled for base metal.
Wording TBC on other versions.

			BU	Proof
2016	(all originally sold in folders/proof sets)		£12.00	£16.00
	3,000 max	.925 sterling silver proof, price new		£82.50
	1,500 max	.925 sterling silver piedfort proof, price new		£155.00
	150 max	.917 gold proof, price new		£1945.00

COMMEMORATIVE TYPE 43
Standard Fifth portrait of QEII
Design by: Jody Clark
House of Windsor
Design by: Timothy Noad
Edge: Milled for base metal.
Wording TBC on other versions.

			BU	Proof
2016	(all originally sold in folders/proof sets)		£12.00	£16.00
		.925 sterling silver proof, price new		TBC
		.925 sterling silver piedfort proof, price new		TBC
		.917 gold proof, price new		TBC

COMMEMORATIVE TYPE 44 - The Queen's Sapphire Jubilee £5 Crown in various base and precious metal guises. Just announced 30/1/17 - no time to include before going to print! New prices similar to type 42.

119

The £20 Coin

A £20 silver coin was first sold in 2013. The first coin has the Pistrucci St. George on the reverse. The 2014 £20 coin shows Britannia with a lion on its reverse. The first 2015 coin features Winston Churchill and second 2015 coin features the new portrait of the Queen, and on the reverse, smaller versions of each of the five portraits used during the Queen's reign. There were three different £20 coins sold in 2016; a coin to mark the Queen's 90th birthday, using the same reverse as the 90th birthday £5 crown, a Welsh Dragon themed coin (originally only available at the Royal Mint in person, but later also sold in different packaging), and a Christmas themed coin.

OBVERSE 1
Coins 1 - 3

They are offered by the Royal Mint for £20.00 plus postage. The value of the silver content is about £6.90 - much lower than the stated face value, which is nothing unusual as the face value of circulating coins has been higher than the material value contained within for centuries. What is confusing though, is the legal tender status of the coin. The coins are not accepted in shops or even at most banks and post offices. See also £50 coin on the next page.

OBVERSE 2
Coins 4 - 7

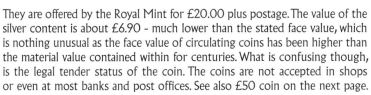

Year	Coin	Price
2013	Coin 1: St. George reverse, 250,000 sold	£23.00*
2014	Coin 2: WWI 1914 1918 Britannia reverse	£23.00*
2015	Coin 3: Winston Churchill reverse	£25.00*
2015	Coin 4: Longest Reign reverse	£25.00*
2016	Coin 5: Queen's 90th reverse	£20.00*
2016	Coin 6: Welsh Dragon reverse (see below)	£35 - £45*
2016	Coin 7: Christmas Nativity scene reverse	£40.00*

* Prices quoted are for coins in original packets. The design used on the 2015 Longest Reign coin was also used for a 5oz silver proof (£395.00 price new, 65mm diameter), 1 kilo silver proof (£2000.00 price new, 100mm) and 1 kilo gold proof coins (price new £42,500.00). The 2016 Welsh Dragon coins were sold at the Royal Mint visitor centre in special packaging and later in different, standard packaging. The coins in the former packaging sell for a little more. 'TWENTY POUNDS' is incorporated under the dragon and therefore is not included in the wording around the Queen.

The £50 Coin

Clearly the £20 coin was quite successful for the Royal Mint Ltd, so the marketing department introduced a £50 coin (and a £100 coin, on the next page). They are approximately half the weight of the £100 coin, but less than twice the weight of the £20 coin. The current bullion value is about £13.65.

Recently a gentleman attempted to pay a total of £29,300 worth of Royal Mint £100 coins in to his bank account. The bank appear to have contacted the mint who it seems were getting more of them back than they cared to receive (and once they are out of their packets and have scratches and scrapes they can't sell them again but still have to recompense the banks), so they issued a memo to the Post Office and to some banks (possibly all banks) in January 2016 telling them not to accept the high value silver (£20, £50 and £100) coins at face value. I warned about a similar potential scenario when the first £20 coin was issued in 2013.

A Royal Mint spokesman says that 'Legal tender allows UK coins to be accepted for payment of debts in court, but only circulating legal tender coins (i.e. the conventional £2 coin and lower values) are designed to be spent and traded at businesses and banks.'

So there is a two-tier legal tender system of circulating coins and non-circulating coins that are legal tender, but aren't really?

As far as I'm concerned these coins are all worth whatever the market is willing to pay for them, and as long as enough people trust the '50 POUNDS' written on them then the values are likely to stay at around that claimed 'face value'.

Britannia Coin   Reverse of Shakespeare Coin

BU

2015	Britannia with lion, in package	£45-£60
2016	Shakespeare theme, in package, price new	£50.00
	Obverse has: ELIZABETH II DG REG FD 50 POUNDS	

The £100 Coin

The Royal Mint made and sold its first £100 coin in 2015. 50,000 of them were sold for £100 each. Currently the silver value is about £27.70 and again, I'm not entirely clear on the true legal tender status of these coins (they seem to only be worth £100 when the owner and any potential buyers believe they are, as long as they don't actually try to spend one! See also notes for the silver £20 and £50 coins). Late 2015 saw the issue of another £100 coin with the new portrait of the Queen and featuring Buckingham palace on its reverse. A new 2016 £100 coin features Trafalgar Square with the lion in the foreground and Nelson's column in the background. Incidentally, the three designs used to date for the £100 coins were also used for three coins of the 'Portrait of Britain (2014 and 2016)' series of £5 crown coins. In crown guise they were Tri-Chromatic pad coloured.

The first £100 Coin (2015)
Standard portrait of Queen Elizabeth II. Design by: Ian Rank-Broadley
The Elizabeth Tower as seen from below. Design by: Glyn Davies and Laura Clancy

The second £100 Coin (2015)
New portrait of QEII with '100 POUNDS 2015'. Design by: Jody Clark
Buckingham Palace with Queen Victoria monument. Design by:
Glyn Davies and Laura Clancy

The third £100 Coin (2016), Not Illustrated
Portrait of QEII with '100 POUNDS 2015'. Design by: Jody Clark
Trafalgar Square. Design by: Glyn Davies and Laura Clancy

			BU
2015	50,000 max	'Big Ben' tower, specimen in folder	£80-£100
2015	50,000 max	Buckingham Palace, specimen in folder	£80-£100
2016	45,000 max	Trafalgar Square, specimen in folder	£85-£100

| 19.41 mm • 3.35 grammes • .925 Silver • edge: milled | SIXPENCE |

The Sixpence

Originally a popular 'old school' coin, first made in 1551 as it was conveniently 1/40th of a Pound and people actually used to spend them, until their demonetisation in 1980 (nearly all coins were made with the sole intention of being spent in those days - crazy isn't it)! It was re-introduced in 2016 to the same size, weight and silver fineness as the pre 1920 sixpences but is now revalued as six new pence instead of six old pence (which is 2.5p in new pence).

I assume these are aimed at the wedding industry - 'something old, something new and a sixpence in her shoe'. Delightful older sixpence coins in perfect condition are often cheaper and readily available from reputable coin dealers, albeit without the fancy paperwork or cumbersome box, which I imagine must be quite uncomfortable when worn in a shoe*.

These are available new for £30.00. Obverse type is the same as the 2015 Britannia £50 coin.

* Recently the sixpence has also been sold in a card pack.

Sixpence -
actual size

Sixpence -
enlarged

United Kingdom Banknotes

The UK currently has four denominations of legal tender banknotes in circulation; the £5, £10, £20 and £50 notes. Some banks in Scotland and in Northern Ireland also issue Sterling banknotes in the same denomination as the Bank of England types (plus the Royal Bank of Scotland continues to issue smaller numbers of £1 notes). These notes are not officially legal tender but they are of course readily accepted within the countries in which they circulate. All of the Scottish and Northern Irish banknotes have to be backed up by Bank of England money; in other words, a bank issuing notes in Scotland or Northern Ireland has to theoretically hold in its vaults the same amount of Bank of England money. Usually this Bank of England money is held in the form of special high-value banknotes that are exchanged just between banks. The circulating Scottish and Northern Ireland banknotes are not covered in this book (perhaps in a future edition).

The four current circulating Bank of England notes are: Paper £5 - Mainly green with Elizabeth Fry on the reverse. Polymer £5 - Mainly green with Winston Churchill on the reverse. £10 - Mainly orange with Charles Darwin on the reverse. £20 - Mainly purple with Adam Smith on the reverse. £50 - Mainly red with Matthew Boulton and James Watt on the reverse.

The 'promise to pay the bearer' on each Bank of England banknote never expires, even when notes of that type have long since been removed from circulation. As a result, every single Bank of England note can always be redeemed for its face value at the Bank of England, and usually at any UK bank. Shopkeepers and other merchants are not obliged to accept older Bank of England notes. Before redeeming older Bank of England notes it's obviously a good idea to check that they don't have a collectable worth first. This can be done using the Rotographic publication "Collectors' Banknotes" which will be published in 2017.

Banknote condition

Just as with coins, condition plays a very important role where the values of banknotes are concerned. Most collectors will attempt to collect the banknotes in the best condition they can afford. With modern banknotes this will nearly always be uncirculated (mint condition) examples, as such examples of modern banknotes are usually obtainable. With this in mind, most well-used, tatty, creased and dirty banknotes that have exchanged hands many times are only likely to be worth their face value. EF is an abbreviation for Extremely Fine and means that a note is in very good condition, but just a little way from being classed as UNCirculated. VF means Very Fine and is quite a common grade for modern notes that have seen limited average use.

Serial numbers

Collectors like interesting serial numbers too. If you ever get given a note with a low serial number, where at least the first 3 digits of the 6 digit number are zeros, keep hold of it. A note with the serial number AH43 000954 will be slightly more interesting than AH43 874563, for example. The note AH43 000001 would of course be more interesting still. AA01 000045 would be even more desirable! Collectors also like interesting patterns in numbers, like AH43 434343, AH22 222222 or AH12 345678. You won't get offered huge amounts of money for notes with interesting serial numbers, but you might persuade someone to give you more than face value, assuming the note is in good condition.

DETAILS

EF   UNC

Signed by <u>Merlyn Lowther</u>, the chief cashier of the Bank of England from 1999 to 2003.

Letter, Letter, Number, Number, followed by 6 digits

	EF	UNC
Number AA01 000000 Special Specimen note		£800.00
HA** followed by 6 digits (special first run)	£6.00	£14.00
HC01 followed by 6 digits (first prefix)	£25.00	£75.00
CL**, DL** or EL** then 6 digits (special column sort prefix)	£10.00	£20.00
XA** to XK** followed by 6 digits (varnish trial prefix)	£200.00	
LL** followed by 6 digits (replacement notes)	£10.00	£20.00
ER50 followed by 6 digits (special presentation pack issue)*		£25
HM02 followed by 6 digits (special presentation pack issue)*		£25
HM03 followed by 6 digits (special presentation pack issue)*		£25
QC03 followed by 6 digits (special presentation pack issue)*		£25
QC50 followed by 6 digits (special presentation pack issue)*		£25
JB** followed by 6 digits (last Lowther prefix)		£10.00

* These notes were only issued as part of special sets.

Banknote images are © Bank of England.

DETAILS   EF   UNC

The first Elizabeth Fry £5 notes bearing the signature of Merlyn Lowther were withdrawn as the serial numbers were not properly varnished and could be partially rubbed off. Initially they were sought after and the extra demand meant they were worth slightly more. The affected notes were taken in, treated and then re released into circulation. None of the original issue now commands a premium.

Signed by <u>Andrew Bailey</u>, the chief cashier of the Bank of England from 2004 to 2011.

Letter, Letter, Number, Number, followed by 6 digits

	EF	UNC
JB** followed by 6 digits (first Bailey prefix)		£10.00
EL02 followed by 6 digits (special column sort prefix)	£10.00	£25.00
EL** followed by 6 digits (special column sort prefix)	£6.00	£12.00
LL** followed by 6 digits (replacement notes)	£10.00	£20.00
LE** followed by 6 digits (last Bailey prefix)		£10.00

Signed by <u>Chris Salmon</u>, the chief cashier of the Bank of England from 2011 to March 2014.

Letter, Letter, Number, Number, followed by 6 digits

	EF	UNC
LE** followed by 6 digits (first Salmon prefix)		£8.00
Later Salmon prefixes LJ** and MD** noted		£8.00

The new polymer £5 note. The red area
shows the transparent window.

DETAILS   **UNC**

The Bank of England are moving from paper notes to polymer (plastic). Polymer notes are harder wearing and harder to fake. The first polymer note, the new £5, was released into circulation on the 13th September 2016. The new notes will circulate along-side the existing paper £5 notes until the old notes are completely removed from circulation in May 2017.

Signed by <u>Victoria Cleland</u>, the chief cashier of the Bank of England from March 2014 to date.

Letter, Letter, Number, Number, followed by 6 digits

AA0I followed by 6 digits (first polymer £5 note prefix) -	
Lower than 000500 serial number	£1,000 - £4,000+
Lower than 100000	£25 - £100
Higher than 100000	£10 - £20
AK47 followed by 6 digits	£6 - £20

As seems to be the norm these days when a new coin or bank note is introduced, there was a predictable frenzy on eBay, especially for AA0I and AK47 notes (because of the rifle with the same designation?!) Quite how many of the eBay sales were to genuine buyers is another matter, but prices went silly nonetheless. The media picked up on it and added further fuel to the silliness. After a few weeks it all came crashing down, as usual, and prices were fairly stable at the time of writing. There will always be demand for AA0I notes, and the lower to serial number the better.

DETAILS	VF	EF	UNC

Signed by <u>Merlyn Lowther</u>, the chief cashier of the Bank of England from 1999 to 2003.

Letter, Letter, Number, Number, followed by 6 digits

Details	VF	EF	UNC
Number AA01 000000 Special Specimen note			£800.00
AA01 followed by 6 digits (first prefix)		£20.00	£50.00*²
AA01 followed by 6 digits (first prefix, worded 'and company')*¹		£30.00	£50.00*²
AD** followed by 6 digits (worded 'and company')*¹		£60.00	£120.00
AH80 followed by 6 digits (last prefix of first type)	£50.00	£150.00	£300.00
AJ01 followed by 6 digits (first production run)		£50.00	£100.00
EL** followed by 6 digits (special column sort prefix)			£20.00
LL** followed by 6 digits (replacement notes)		£75.00	£150.00
LL** followed by 6 digits (replacement notes 'and company')*		£40.00	£90.00
CC80 followed by 6 digits (highest prefix known*²)	£20.00	£75.00	£150.00
MH**, MJ**, MK**, MM** (experimental notes)	£100.00	£150.00	
ER50 followed by 6 digits (special presentation pack issue)*			£30.00
QC50 followed by 6 digits (special presentation pack issue)*			£30.00
QV10 followed by 6 digits (special presentation pack issue)*			£30.00
VR10 followed by 6 digits (special presentation pack issue)*			£30.00

* These notes were only issued as part of special sets.

*¹ These notes have the wording 'The Governor and Company of the Bank of England' in the band of text above the central oval where the Queen's watermark appears. A variety exists with the wording 'The Governor <u>and the</u> Company of the Bank of England'. Both types were made in high numbers.

*² Very low serial numbers will be worth more.

Banknote images are © Bank of England.

*² The CC** prefix overlaps with the CC** Bailey notes below. Until recently it was thought that CC40 was the last Lowther prefix. This is not that case as prefixes up to CC80 have been noted on Lowther notes.

DETAILS	EF	UNC

Signed by <u>Andrew Bailey</u>, the chief cashier of the Bank of England from 2004 to 2011.

Letter, Letter, Number, Number, followed by 6 digits

	EF	UNC
CC41 followed by 6 digits (lowest known prefix)	£60.00	£120.00
EL** followed by 6 digits (special column sort prefix)	£15.00	£25.00
EL80 followed by 6 digits (last column sort EL prefix)	£50.00	£100.00
HL01 followed by 6 digits (first column sort HL prefix)	£50.00	£100.00
HL** followed by 6 digits (special column sort prefix)	£20.00	£50.00
LL** followed by 6 digits (replacement notes)	£15.00	£35.00
LA** followed by 6 digits (last Bailey prefix)	£15.00	£35.00

Signed by <u>Chris Salmon</u>, the chief cashier of the Bank of England from 2011 to March 2014.

Letter, Letter, Number, Number, followed by 6 digits

	EF	UNC
Prefix JH** followed by 6 digits (first Salmon prefix)		£14.00
Later Salmon prefixes		£14.00

Signed by <u>Victoria Cleland</u>, the chief cashier of the Bank of England from March 2014 to date.

Letter, Letter, Number, Number, followed by 6 digits

	EF	UNC
Prefix LH** followed by 6 digits (first Cleland prefix)	£12.00	£25.00
Later Cleland prefixes		£14.00

Polymer £10 notes will be introduced by Summer 2017.

Banknote images are © Bank of England.

DETAILS	EF	UNC

Signed by <u>Andrew Bailey</u>, the chief cashier of the Bank of England from 2004 to 2011.

Letter, Letter, Number, Number, followed by 6 digits

	EF	UNC
AA01 followed by 6 digits (first Bailey prefix)	£50.00	£200.00*
AA** followed by 6 digits (first Bailey prefix)	£25.00	£38.00
AL** followed by 6 digits (special column sort prefix)	£25.00	£38.00
LL** followed by 6 digits (replacement notes)	£30.00	£50.00
HD36 followed by 6 digits (last Bailey prefix)		£38.00

* Very low serial numbers will be worth more.

Signed by <u>Chris Salmon</u> the chief cashier of the Bank of England from 2011 to March 2014.

Letter, Letter, Number, Number, followed by 6 digits

	EF	UNC
HA** followed by 6 digits (first Salmon prefix)		£30.00
Mid Salmon prefixes		£26.00
JH** followed by 6 digits (last Salmon prefix)		£30.00

Signed by <u>Victoria Cleland</u> the chief cashier of the Bank of England from March 2014 to date.

Letter, Letter, Number, Number, followed by 6 digits

	EF	UNC
JH** followed by 6 digits (first Cleland prefix)		£35.00
Later Cleland prefixes		£28.00

Polymer £20 notes will be introduced by 2020.

Banknote images are © Bank of England.

DETAILS UNC

Signed by <u>Chris Salmon,</u> the chief cashier of the Bank of England from 2011 to March 2014.

Letter, Number, Number, followed by 6 digits

AA** followed by 6 digits (first prefix)	£85.00*
Mid Salmon prefixes	£70.00
AJ** followed by 6 digits (last prefix)	£85.00

*Very low AA01 notes are worth more.

Signed by <u>Victoria Cleland,</u> the chief cashier of the Bank of England from March 2014 to date.

Letter, Number, Number, followed by 6 digits

AJ** followed by 6 digits (first prefix)	£85.00
Later Cleland prefixes (noted to AK**)	£70.00

Chief Cashier Signatures on Current Bank of England notes

Merlyn Lowther, Chief Cashier 1999 - 2003
(her signature can be seen on the oldest,
but still current £5 and £10 notes)

Dr Andrew John Bailey,
Chief Cashier 2004 - 2011
(his signature can be seen on some current
£5, £10 and £20 notes)

Chris Salmon, Chief Cashier 2011 - 2014
(his signature can be seen on some current
£5, £10, £20 and £50 notes)

Victoria Cleland, Chief Cashier 2014 to date
(her signature can be seen on the newest
£10, £20 and £50 notes and the polymer
£5 notes)

From 1971 to 1982, The Royal Mint issued proof coin sets sealed in plastic, enclosed in lightweight card envelopes. The coins within often tone badly over time and the card outer case is sometimes worse for wear. Values at the upper end of the ranges shown below are usually for sets in very good condition. Values fluctuate and sets can often be purchased for less and sometimes they sell for more, especially as gifts for round birthday's, so expect 1977, 1987 and 1997 to potentially climb in value a little during 2017.

Year	No. of Coins.	Price New*	Notes	Value
1971	6	£3.15		£5 - £10
1972	7	£3.30	Inc. Crown	£13 - £20
1973	6	£5.90		£6 - £14
1974	6	£5.90		£6 - £14
1975	6	£5.90		£6 - £12
1976	6	£5.90		£6 - £12
1977	7	£8.30	Inc. Crown	£6 - £12
1978	6	£6.40		£6 - £12
1979	6	£6.40		£8 - £12
1980	6	£8.30		£5 - £10
1981	6	£9.40		£8 - £12
1982	7	£7.50	20p added	£6 - £12

In 1983, the packaging was changed to a blue leatherette bookshelf type case.

Year	No. of Coins.	Price New*	Notes	Value
1983	8	£15.60	£1 added	£9 - £14
1984	8	£17.20		£8 - £14

From 1985 onward, two types of packaging were offered: The "standard" blue leatherette case, and the "deluxe" red leather case. Values don't tend to be vastly different.

Year	No. of Coins.	Price New*	Notes	Value
1985	7	£20.60		£6 - £15
1986	8	£17.10	Inc. commem. £2	£6 - £15
1987	7	£16.50		£6 - £12
1988	7	£13.40		£6 - £15
1989	9	£16.20	Inc. both £2	£25 - £30
1990	8	£17.15		£6 - £15
1991	7	£16.45		£6 - £15
1992	9	£22.25	2x 10p, 2x 50p	£35 - £50
1993	8	£33.30	Inc. Crown	£10 - £20
1994	8	£29.00	Inc. commem £2	£12 - £20
1995	8	£29.00?		£12 - £20
1996	9	£28.90		£17 - £26
1997	10	£30.00?		£15 - £25
1998	10	£35.50		£15 - £25
1999	9	£31.25		£15 - £25
2000	10	£34.50		£20 - £30

* Original printed material with price data was hard to find. The prices shown are the prices that the sets were originally sold for in the USA, converted to GBP at the then exchange rate - source 'Standard Catalog of World Coins' published by KP books. If you have original printed advertising material or old receipts etc that show the original UK prices of any of the proof sets, particularly the missing ones on the next page, please get in touch!

From 2001 on, it is accepted that all sets will contain the standard 8 pieces: 1p, 2p, 5p, 10p, 20p, 50p, £1, and £2. The Royal Mint, also produced deluxe proof sets and executive proof sets, which all contain the same coins but have better packaging. The deluxe and executive sets are sometimes sold for up to 20% more than the standard sets.

Sets that include currently higher priced coins (e.g. the 2009 set containing the Kew Gardens 50p) are priced higher than others, which is a little odd really, as the numbers of proof sets (and therefore proof coins) made is generally around the same - approximately 35,000 sets were sold in 2009, which is about the same as the number of sets sold in 2008, but just because the 2008 set doesn't include a 'special' coin, it's worth well over £100 less. Proof coins are of course very different to their normal circulation counterparts, but in general they don't seem to be viewed as different types of coins by the public, but rather as higher quality versions of the normal coins.

Recently 'Premium' sets have been introduced which include a medallion. In 2013 the Royal Mint made the proof sets available in reduced size 'definitive' form, which include just the standard 1p to £2, a 'commemorative' set which is just the commemorative 50p, £1, £2 and £5 coins and also a complete set made up of all the coins. I'm starting to lose track, and I honestly don't think the packaging will play much of a roll in the future - the coins are what they are, regardless of the current sales/packaging strategy! Obviously the definitive and commemorative 'short' sets are worth less than the full sets. They now also sell silver proof sets of all of the annual coins, silver proof sets of just the commemorative coins, silver proof piedfort sets of just the commemorative coins and gold proof sets of just the commemorative coins!

If the various types of packaging, alloys and coin configurations weren't confusing enough, the annual proof sets no longer necessarily actually contain all of the coins from a given year. For example there are no sets that contain the 2015 5th portrait Battle of Britain 50p, 5th portrait 2015 Royal Navy £2 or 5th portrait 2015 Magna Carta £2. Also, the 2016 proof sets contain none of the five Beatrix Potter 2016 50p coins.

Year	No. of Coins.	Price New*	Notes	Value
2001	10	£34.50		£20 - £28
2002	9	£30.00		£20 - £30
2003	11	£31.25		£20 - £30
2004	10	£ ?		£20 - £30
2005	12	£ ?		£35 - £50
2006	13	£ ?		£30 - £50
2007	12	£ ?		£30 - £40
2008	11	£ ?		£30 - £40
2009	12	£ ?		£160 - £200
2010	13	£ ?		£30 - £45
2011	14	£ ?		£90 - £110
2012	10	£ ?		£40 - £60
2013	15	£ ?		£130 - £150
2014	14	£ ?		£170 - £200
2015	13	£ ?		£100 - £130
2016	16	£ ?		£170 - £220
2017	13	£145.00		

1982 Proof set, resting on it's card outer and certificate
- pre 1980 sets did not include a certificate.

1985 Proof set in standard blue leatherette, from
above with certificate. The blue and red mid 1980s
to late 1990s cases can also be opened like this to
aid display.

1988 Deluxe Proof set in red leather case.

2003 Standard Proof set in red box - early 2000s standard sets were sold in either blue or red boxes like this.

In 1982, the Royal Mint introduced Brilliant Uncirculated sets, which contain most of the coins contained in the Proof sets (crowns normally not included). These sets do not have proof-quality striking, and are packaged in a folder style with text to provide historic background information and specifications of the coins.

Year	Pieces	Coins	Notes
1982	7	½p, 1p, 2p, 5p, 10p, 20p, 50p	
1983	8	½p, 1p, 2p, 5p, 10p, 20p, 50p, £1	new £1 added
1984	8	½p, 1p, 2p, 5p, 10p, 20p, 50p, £1	
1985	7	1p, 2p, 5p, 10p, 20p, 50p, £1	½p removed
1986	8	1p, 2p, 5p, 10p, 20p, 50p, £1, £2	Commonwealth Games
1987	7	1p, 2p, 5p, 10p, 20p, 50p, £1	
1988	7	1p, 2p, 5p, 10p, 20p, 50p, £1	
1989	7	1p, 2p, 5p, 10p, 20p, 50p, £1	
1990	8	1p, 2p, 5p, 5p, 10p, 20p, 50p, £1	Large & small 5p
1991	7	1p, 2p, 5p, 10p, 20p, 50p, £1	
1992	9	1p, 2p, 5p, 10p, 10p, 20p, 50p, 50p, £1	lg & sm 10p; EEC 50p
1993	8	1p, 2p, 5p, 10p, 20p, 50p, £1, £5	Coronation Anniversary
1994	8	1p, 2p, 5p, 10p, 20p, 50p, £1, £2	Bank of England
1995	8	1p, 2p, 5p, 10p, 20p, 50p, £1, £2	Dove of Peace
1996	8	1p, 2p, 5p, 10p, 20p, 50p, £1, £2	Football
1997	9	1p, 2p, 5p, 10p, 20p, 50p, 50p, £1, £2	Large & small 50p
1998	9	1p, 2p, 5p, 10p, 20p, 50p, 50p, £1, £2	EU
1999	8	1p, 2p, 5p, 10p, 20p, 50p, £1, £2	Rugby £2 (no normal £2)
2000	9	1p, 2p, 5p, 10p, 20p, 50p, 50p, £1, £2	Public Libraries
2001	9	1p, 2p, 5p, 10p, 20p, 50p, £1, £2, £2	Marconi
2002	8	1p, 2p, 5p, 10p, 20p, 50p, £1, £2	
2003	10	1p, 2p, 5p, 10p, 20p, 50p, 50p, £1, £2, £2	Women's Suffrage, DNA
2004	10	1p, 2p, 5p, 10p, 20p, 50p, 50p, £1, £2, £2	Bannister, Trevithick
2005	10	1p, 2p, 5p, 10p, 20p, 50p, 50p, £1, £2, £2	Dictionary, Guy Fawkes
2006	10	1p, 2p, 5p, 10p, 20p, 50p, 50p, £1, £2, £2	Victoria Cross, Brunel
2007	9	1p, 2p, 5p, 10p, 20p., 50p, £1, £2, £2	Slave trade, Act of Union
2008	7	1p - £1 old designs 'Emblems of Britain'	
2008	7	1p - £1 new designs	
2008	14	1p - £1 both designs	
2008	9	1p, 2p, 5p, 10p, 20p, 50p, £1, £2, £2	Old designs. Olympic £2.
2009	11	1p, 2p, 5p, 10p, 20p, 50p, 50p, £1, £2, £2, £2	Kew, Burns, Darwin.
2010	8	1p, 2p, 5p, 10,p 20p, 50p, £1, £2	
2011	13	1p, 2p, 5p, 10p, 20p, 50p, 50p, £1 x3, £2 x3	

Year	Pieces	Coins	Notes
2011	13	1p, 2p, 5p, 10p, 20p, 50p, 50p, £1 x3, £2 x3	
2012	10	1p, 2p, 5p, 10p, 20p, 50p, £1, £2, £2, £5	
2013	15	1p, 2p, 5p, 10p, 20p, 50p x2, £1 x3, £2 x4, £5	
2014	14	1p, 2p, 5p, 10p, 20p, 50p x2, £1 x3, £2 x3, £5	
2015	13	1p, 2p, 5p, 10p, 20p, 50p x2, £1, £2 x3, £5 x2	
2016	16	1p, 2p, 5p, 10p, 20p, 50p x2, £1 x2, £2 x6, £5	£55 price new
2017	13	1p,.2p, 5p, 10p, 20p, 50p x2, £1, £2 x3, £5 x2	£55 price new

The BU sets tend to sell from between 2.5x to 5x the face value of the coins included. Sets in mint condition with absolutely no toning on any of the coins will attract a premium. Some sets are affected by the current higher prices of some of the coins contained within, for example the 2009 set is affected by the Kew Gardens 50p frenzy and values for that one are about £150. See 50p Commemorative Type 13 for further details. 106,332 of the 2009 set were sold.

Recently BU sets of 'definitive' coins have also been sold, which just contain the standard 1p to £2 coins and no commemoratives. Over the years there have also been other packaging options included a baby theme and wedding theme.

The sets below were specially marketed for commemorative or promotional purposes. Other later sets exist and may be included in a future edition. To be honest though, they aren't really incredibly popular and the total value is usually based strongly on the sum of the value of the coins within.

1983	7	½p, 1p, 2p, 5p, 10p, 20p, 50p
		Specially packaged set for the H J Heinz Company.
1983	8	½p, 1p, 2p, 5p, 10p, 20p, 50p, £1
		Specially packaged set for the Martini & Rossi Company.
1988	7	1p, 2p, 5p, 10p, 20p, 50p, £1
		Special package celebrating Australia's Bicentennial.
1996	14	1p, 2p, 5p, 10p, 20p, 50p, £1; pre-decimal 1/2d, 1d, 3d, 6d, 1/, 2/, 2/6d
	(7+7)	Special package commemorating 25 years of decimalisation.
2000	9	1p,2p,5p,10p,20p,50p,£1,£2, £5 (Millennium)
		In special "Time Capsule" packaging.
2004	3	50p (Roger Bannister), £1 (Forth bridge), £2 (Trevithick's Locomotive)
		"Celebrating Human Achievement"
2005	3	50p (Johnson's dictionary), £1 (Menai bridge), £2 (Guy Fawkes)
		new packaging of commemorative issues

The following are sterling (.925) silver proof sets, designed for various occasions, including the introduction of the coins themselves. These are normally found in hard acrylic capsules, enclosed in a clam-shell case, and with a certificate from the Royal Mint. Some issues post 1998 are included in the main section.

Please note that the coins and sets of coins on the following four pages are not necessarily exhaustive. The pairs and sets of coins in particular have been issued in an almost random fashion over the years and tend to have sold new in fairly low numbers. On the second hand market years later there are very few, if any, that are worth substantially more than the total value of the coins contained within.

Five Pence

1990	35,000	large & small sized pair	£25.00

Ten Pence

1992	35,000	large & small sized pair	£25.00

Fifty Pence

1997	10,304	large & small sized pair	£25.00
1998	22,078	NHS issue and EU issue pair	£55.00
1998		pair, EU silver proof & EU silver Piedfort	£70.00

One Pound

1983 - 88	1,000	set of 6 regional designs, Arms, Shield	£75.00
1984 - 87	50,000	set of 4 regional designs	£90.00
1994 - 97	25,000	set of 4 regional designs	£100.00
1999 - 2002	25,000	set of 4 regional designs	£100.00

Two Pounds

1989	25,000	Bill of Rights & Claim of Rights pair	£60.00
1997	40,000	new bi-metallic circulation issue	£20.00
1998	25,000	new portrait on the circulation issue	£20.00
1997/98		bi-metallic Maklouf & Rank-Broadley pair	£35.00

ALERT

It seems that official Royal Mint cases were once obtainable, and some sets were assembled on the secondary market, with the individual coins and accompanying certificates. Original RM-issued sets usually contain a single certificate, listing each coin in the set.

1981	5,000	set, all issues, 1/2p-50p in base metals, sterling 25p commemorative, 22k gold Sovereign & £5	£700.00
1981		pair, sterling 25p commemorative, 22k gold Sovereign	£250.00
1992	1,000	set, both lg and sm 10p, 50p EEC, and £1	£75.00
1993	1,000	set, 50p EEC, £1, and £5 Coronation commem.	£75.00
1994	2,000	set, 50p D-Day, £1, and £2 Bank of England	£70.00
1995	1,000	silver set, peace £2, UN £2 and £1 coin	£50.00
1996	1,000	silver set, £5, £2 and £1 coins	£50.00
1996		set, all issues, 1p-£1 (25th Anniversary of Decimalisation)	£70.00
	500	pair, 1996 70th Birthday crown & 1997 Royal Wedding Jubilee crown	£60.00
1997		set, 50p, £1, £2, £5 Wedding Jubilee, £2 Britannia	£120.00
1999		set, £5 Millennium, £2 Britannia	£40.00
1999		set, £2 Britannia, £10 stamp	
2000	13,180	set, 1p-£5 Millennium, plus Maundy set (13 pieces)	£200.00
2000		£5 Millennium, plus YR2000 serial numbered £20 note	
		pair, 2002 Silver Jubilee crown & 2003 Coronation Jubilee crown	£60.00
2004		pair, 2004 Entente Cordiale crown & French €1 1/2 commem.	£75.00
2004	750	set, 50p Bannister, £1 Forth Bridge, £2 Trevithick, £5 Entente Cordiale £2 Britannia.	£75.00
-		1999, 2001, 2002, 2003 £2 Britannia uncirculated.	£80.00
2005		Pair of silver proof £5 coins - Nelson and Trafalgar	£65.00
2008		Set of 14 £1 coins, all designs 1983 to 2008. All dated 2008 with gold plated details	£300.00
2015		Silver proof set of definitive coins with the new portrait of the Queen, price new	£240.00

The following set was struck in .917 (22K) gold.

2002	2,002	set, 1p-£5 Golden Jubilee, plus Maundy set (13 pieces)	£750.00

Values of later sets including various combinations of coins that the Royal Mint offer tend to be worth about the same as the sum of the individual coins they contain.

Piedforts are coins that are double the thickness and weight of the normal version, and are almost always struck in sterling (.925) silver. These are normally found in hard acrylic capsules, enclosed in a clam-shell case, and with a certificate from the Royal Mint.

Five Pence

1990	20,000	.925 sterling silver, small size Piedfort	£20.00

Ten Pence

1992		.925 sterling silver, small size Piedfort	£30.00

Twenty Pence

1982		.925 sterling silver, Piedfort	£30.00

Fifty Pence

1997	7,192	.925 sterling silver, small size Piedfort	£50.00
1998		EEC & NHS pair, Piedfort	£30.00
1992/3 & 1998		.925 sterling silver Piedfort of both EU related coins	£85.00

One Pound

1983 - 88	500	set of 6 regional designs, Arms, Shield, Piedfort	£250.00
1984 - 87	10,000	.925 sterling silver, proof set of 4 Piedfort	£175.00
1994 - 97	10,000	.925 sterling silver, proof set of 4 Piedfort	£190.00
1999-2002	10,000	.925 sterling silver, proof set of 4 Piedfort	£225.00
2004-2007	1,400	.925 sterling silver, proof set of 4 Piedfort	£200.00

Two Pounds

1989	10,000	Bill of Rights & Claim of Rights pair, Piedfort	£30.00
1997	10,000	.925 sterling silver, Piedfort	£55.00
1998	10,000	.925 sterling silver, Piedfort £55	
1997/98	.10,000	925 sterling silver, Piedfort (pair)	£125.00
1999	10,000	.925 sterling silver, proof Piedfort HOLOGRAM	£100.00

Five Pounds

2005		Nelson & Trafalgar pair, Piedfort	£125.00

Sets

2003		set, 50p WPSU, £1 Royal Arms, £2 DNA Piedfort	£60.00
2004	7500	set, 50p Bannister, £1 Forth Bridge, £2 Trevithick Piedfort	£150.00
2005		set, 50p Johnson's Dictionary, £1 Menai Bridge, £2 Gunpowder Plot, £2 World War II Piedfort	£150.00
2007		£5, both £2 coins, £1 and 50p Piedfort	£250.00
2008		2x £5 coins, £2 and £1 Piedfort	£250.00
2008		The 7 new Dent design coins as silver Piedforts	£350.00
2009		Piedfort gold proof set of 16x difference 50 pence's	£ EXPENSIVE
2010		£5, £2, both £1 coins and the 50p	£300.00

Sets

2010/2011	Capital cities 4x £1 set	£300.00
2013	4x £5 coins, each with different Queen portrait	£683.00 new price
2013	The 5 Commemorative coins + the 2 £1 coins	£560.00 new price
2013	Pair of London Underground £2 coins	£200.00 new price
2014	The 4 Commemorative coins + the 2 £1 coins	£575.00 new price
2015	The 5 Commemorative coins	£570.00 new price

Special Collector Issues (Patterns)

A trial bi-metallic piece was issued in 1994 (predecessor to the £2 bi-metallic). The obverse shows a cutty (ship), while the reverse carries the Maklouf portrait of QEII. The ring bears the legend "ROYAL MINT TRIAL PATTERN", and an edge legend of 'ANNO REGNIA XLVI, DECUS ET TUTAMEN". See the £2 section.

Pattern sets issued by the Royal Mint to preview the new issue of "Bridges" £1 coins. All of these coins carry the date of 2003, and rather than having a face value, they are labelled as "PATTERN".

2003	7,500	.925 sterling silver, 7,500 , proof set of 4	£80.00
	3,000	.917 gold proof set of 4	£1500.00

A continuation of the above set, this set shows the "Beasts" series, which was a runner-up in the design competition for the new £1 coinage. All of these coins carry the date of 2004, and rather than having a face value, they are labelled as "PATTERN". Issued, as listed, in both sterling (.925) silver, and 22k (.917) gold.

2004	5,000	.925 sterling silver, proof set of 4	£90.00
	2,250	.917 gold proof set of 4	£1500.00
2015		Trial 12-sided £1 coin - see £1 section.	

143

Silver Britannia issues began in 1997 with proof-only coins. Commencing in 1998, originally the Royal Mint followed a pattern of using the standard Standing Britannia for every other year (even years), while bringing out new unique designs for the odd years. These coins were struck in Britannia silver (.9584 fine) which I thought was the whole point - coins featuring Britannia made of Britannia silver. From 2013 onwards they were struck in .999 silver and the diameter has been reduced from 40mm to 38.61mm. Also from 2013 the Royal Mint introduced privy marks (on the edge) and also larger 5oz silver coins, the latter are not included in this book. From 2016 the new Jody Clark bust replaced the Ian Rank-Broadley bust of the queen.

In 2014 the RM introduced another bullion range of coins, in .999 silver and also in .9999 gold. According to the blurb, they: 'Celebrating Chinese and British heritage with a dynamic design'. The silver 1oz versions are also 38.61mm in diameter.

In 2016 the RM introduced another bullion range of coins called the Queen's Beasts. There are eight different sizes (combined across gold and silver issues), most are available in proof form and some are available as just 'bullion' issues. It all seems rather complicated and they seem very much aimed at the bullion market and less so for coin collectors. I suspect they are placed to compete with other international bullion coin issues. They are not included in this book as I feel I need to fill the space with the coins that most people see every day, rather than the seemingly never-ending array of specialist Royal Mint coin issues that appeal less to the masses.

Bullion Silver (UNC) £2 issues

Year	Mintage	Description	Value
1998	88,909	Standing Britannia (Reverse 2)	£23.00
1999	69,394	Britannia in Chariot (Reverse 1)	£23.00
2000	81,301	Standing Britannia (Reverse 2)	£28.00
2001	44,816	Una & the Lion (Reverse 3)	£40.00
2002	48,215	Standing Britannia (Reverse 2)	£30.00
2003	73,271	Helmeted Britannia facing left (Reverse 4)	£28.00
2004	100,000	Standing Britannia (Reverse 2)	£30.00
2005	100,000	Britannia seated (Reverse 5)	£50.00
2006	100,000	Standing Britannia (Reverse 2)	£30.00
2007	100,000	Britannia seated (Reverse 6)	£40.00
2008	100,000	Standing Britannia (not illustrated)	£25.00
2009	100,000	Britannia in Chariot (Reverse 1)	£28.00
2010	126,367	Bust of Britannia in profile (not illustrated)	£20.00
2011	100,000	Seated Britannia (not illustrated)	£20.00
2012	100,000	Standing Britannia (Reverse 2)	£20.00
2013		Reverse 2 (exists with snake privy mark#)	£20.00
2014		Reverse 2 (exists with horse privy mark#)	£20.00
2014		Mule error, with Lunar coin obverse (missing edge dentils)*	£80.00
2015		Standing Britannia (Reverse 2)	£20.00
2015		As above, with privy mark#	Scarce
2016		Standing Britannia (Reverse 2)	£20.00

* Not Illustrated. # Snake mintage est. 300,000. Horse est. 1,000,000. Goat est. 200,000

Silver (PROOF) issues (Reverse types from 1998 - 2012 are the same as pevious)

Year	Denom	Mintage	Notes	Price
1997	£2	4,173	Britannia in Chariot (Reverse 1)	£130.00
	20p	8,686	Both with Raphael Maklouf Bust	£20.00
1998	£2	2,168		£70.00
	20p	2,724		£20.00
2001	£2	3,047		£60.00
	20p	826		£20.00
2003	£2	1,833		£60.00
	20p	1,003		£20.00
2004	£2	5,000		£120.00
2005	£2	2,500		£60.00
2006	£2	2,500	With gold plated details	£130.00
2007	£2	5,147		£60.00
2008	£2	2,500		£60.00
	20p	725		£30.00
2009	£2	6,784		£60.00
	£1	2,500		£30.00
	50p	2,500		£20.00
	20p	3,500		£20.00
2010	£2	6,539		£50.00
	£1	3,497		£20.00
	50p	3,497		£20.00
	20p	4,486		£20.00
2011	£2	4,973		£50.00
	£1	2,483		£20.00
	50p	2,483		£20.00
	20p	2,483		£20.00
2012	£2	2,937		£50.00
2013	£10	4,054	From here on, reverses are not the same as	£300.00+?
	£2	3,468	those used on the bullion series (not illustrated)	£70.00
	20p			£30.00
	10p			£20.00

Britannia
Reverse 1

Britannia
Reverse 2

Britannia
Reverse 3

2014	£10		(not illustrated) Price new	£300.00+?
	£2			£70.00
2015	£10	650 max	(not illustrated*) Price new	£395.00
	£2	3000 max		£75.00
2016	£10		(not illustrated) Price new	£300.00+?
	£2	4150 max		£85.00

Britannia - Obverse type used 1998 - 2015	Britannia Reverse 4	Britannia Reverse 5

Britannia Reverse 6   The Lunar series 2014 Horse

Lunar series 2015 Sheep (obverse as 2014 Horse coin)   The Lunar series 2016 Monkey

Special (PROOF) sets

1997	11,832	Set of 4 (£2, £1, 50p, 20p)	£140.00
1998	3,044	Set of 4 (£2, £1, 50p, 20p)	£140.00
2001	4,596	Set of 4 (£2, £1, 50p, 20p)	£130.00
2003	3,623	Set of 4 (£2, £1, 50p, 20p)	£130.00
2005	5,000	Set of 4 (£2, £1, 50p, 20p)	£140.00
2006	-	Set of 5x different £2 with gold plated details	£250.00
2007	2,500	Set of 4 (£2, £1, 50p, 20p)	£130.00
2007		Set of 6 different £1 proofs	£140.00
2008		Set of 4 (£2, £1, 50p, 20p)	£130.00
2009		Set of 4 (£2, £1, 50p, 20p)	£130.00
2010		Set of 4 (£2, £1, 50p, 20p)	£130.00
2011		Set of 4 (£2, £1, 50p, 20p)	£150.00
2012		Set of 4 (£2, £1, 50p, 20p)	£150.00
2013	Now in .999 silver	Set of 5 (£2, £1, 50p, 20p, 10p)	£150.00
		Pair of 20p and 10p	£37.50 new price
2014		Set of 5	£200.00
2015			

Platinum 2007 Coins were issued to mark the 20th Anniversary of the 'Britannia'

2007	£10		1/10 oz Platinum	£200.00
2007	£25		1/4 oz Platinum	£450.00
2007		250	Set of 4 Platinum coins	£3000.00

Lunar coins, proof issue prices (bullion versions tend to sell for about 2-2.5x bullion value)

2014	Horse design, 1 ounce proof .999 Silver see previous page for picture	£82..50
	Mule error,* with Britannia coin obverse (edge dentils present)	£80.00
	Horse, 5 ounce proof .999 silver	£300.00
	Horse, 1 ounce proof .9999 gold	£1500.00
2015	Sheep, 1 ounce proof .999 silver	£82.50
	Sheep, Tenth of an ounce proof .9999 gold	£200.00
	Sheep, 1 ounce proof .999 silver (gold plated)	£110.00
	Sheep, 1 ounce proof .9999 gold	£1950.00
	Sheep, 5 ounce proof .999 silver	£350.00
	Sheep, 5 ounce proof .9999 gold	£7500.00
2016	Monkey, 1 ounce .999 silver	£82.50
	Monkey, Tenth of an ounce proof .9999 gold	£175.00
	Monkey, 1 ounce proof .9999 gold	£1450.00
	Monkey, 5 ounce proof .999 Silver	£395.00
	Monkey, 5 ounce proof .9999 gold	£7500.00
	Monkey, 1kg proof, .999 silver	£2000.00
	Monkey, 1kg proof, .9999 gold	£42,500.00

All lunar reverse designs are by Wuon-Gean Ho. * Est. mintage 33,000.

147

Gold Britannia issues began in 1987, as both bullion issues as well as proof issues. The values of the bullion issues are based on the value of the gold content, which fluctuates daily. The prices for these issues are given only as a guideline.

Bullion .917 Gold (UNC) Issues

£10	tenth ounce	Bullion Value + 30 to 50%
£25	quarter ounce	Bullion Value + 12 to 25%
£50	half ounce	Bullion Value + 8 to 20%
£100	one ounce	Bullion Value + 5 to 15%

The following are 4-piece sets, each coin encapsulated, and housed in a clamshell case,.

Special PROOF sets of 4 coins (for some dates, 3 or 5 coin sets were issued)

1987	10,000	Britannia standing	£2100.00
1988	3,505	Britannia standing	£2100.00
1989	2,268	Britannia standing	£2300.00
1990	527	Britannia standing	£2500.00
1991	509	Britannia standing	£2500.00
1992	500	Britannia standing	£2300.00
1993	462	Britannia standing	£2300.00
1994	435	Britannia standing	£2300.00
1995	500	Britannia standing	£2300.00
1996	483	Britannia standing	£2300.00
1997	892	Britannia standing	£2300.00
1998	750	Britannia standing	£2300.00
1999	750	Britannia standing	£2250.00
2000	750	Britannia standing	£2300.00
2001	1,000	Una & the Lion	£2300.00
2002	945	Britannia standing	£2300.00
2003	1,250	Britannia with Helmet	£2300.00
2004	973	Britannia standing	£2300.00
2005	1,439	Britannia seated	£2300.00
2006	1,163	Britannia standing	£2300.00
2007	1,250	Britannia seated	£2300.00
2008	1,250	Britannia standing	£2300.00
2009	797 max	Britannia standing in chariot	£2300.00
2010	867 max	Britannia bust in profile	£2500.00
2011	698 max	4 coin set	£2500.00
		3 coin set	£1300.00
2012	352	Britannia standing 4 coin set	£2200.00
	99	3 coin set	£1000.00?
2013	261	Now .9999 gold	£2900.00 new price
	136+90 premium	3 coin set	£700.00
2014		6 coin set	£2600.00 new price
		3 coin set	£1175.00 new price

148

2015	250 max	6 coin set	£2,895.00 new price
	250 max	3 coin set	£350.00 new price
2016	175 max	6 coin set	£3,175.00 new price
	70 max	3 coin premium set	£1,450 new price

Britannia (PROOF) individual cased coins

£100	1997	£1200.00
£100	Other dates	£1000.00-£1200.00
£50	All dates	£550.00-£650.00
£25	All dates	£300.00-£400.00
£10	All dates	Around £130.00-£170.00

Britannia (PROOF) platinum cased coins

£10	All dates	Around £200.00-£230.00
£25	2007 Noted	Arround £400.00

Values of platinum Britannia coins tend to be as much as 4x the metal value. In comparison to the gold and silver issues, they are not often offered for sale.

The Queen's Beasts

In 2016 the Royal Mint introduced the Queen's Beasts series. There are eight different sizes (combined across gold and silver issues). This book aims to focus on actual coins, rather than the ever diversifying range of gold and silver coins that are not really coins at all in the strictest sense.

Gold Sovereign-based single coins are defined as non-commemorative Five Pounds, Two Pounds, Sovereigns and Half Sovereigns struck to normal or proof standards and sold singularly as gold bullion coins or as proof collectors' coins. The non-proof coins do not have boxes or certificates and are normally just traded as gold. Sovereigns and half sovereigns are 22 carat gold (.917 fine) and weigh 7.98g and 3.97g respectively.

Five Pounds

1984	Cased proof only	£1300.00
1984	Cased proof only with 'U' in circle next to date	£1200.00
1985	Cased proof only	£1300.00
1985	with 'U' in circle next to date	£1200.00
1986	with 'U' in circle next to date	£1300.00
1987	with 'U' in circle next to date	£1300.00
1988	with 'U' in circle next to date	£1300.00
1989	Sovereign Anniversary type (on it's own, from a set)	£2800.00
1989	Sovereign Anniversary type, cased proof	£3200.00
1990	with 'U' in circle next to date	£1300.00
1991	with 'U' in circle next to date	£1300.00
1992	with 'U' in circle next to date	£1300.00
1993	with 'U' in circle next to date	£1300.00
1994	with 'U' in circle next to date	£1300.00
1995	with 'U' in circle next to date	£1300.00
1996	with 'U' in circle next to date	£1300.00
1997	with 'U' in circle next to date	£1300.00
1998	New portrait	£1300.00
1999		£1300.00
2000		£1300.00
2000	with 'U' in circle next to date	£1300.00
2001		£1300.00
2002	Shield reverse	£1300.00
2003 to 2010		£1300.00
2011		£1400.00
2012		£1400.00
2013 to 2015		£1800.00

Two Pounds (double sovereign)

All are cased proofs. The £2 coin has not often been issued on its own.

1987		£600.00
1988		£600.00
1989	Sovereign Anniversary type	£9500.00
1990		£600.00
1991		£600.00
1992		£600.00
1993		£600.00
1994	(see 1994 error commemorative type 4 £2 coin)	
1996		£600.00
2014	In connection with birth of Prince George, price new	£650.00

Sovereigns, loose bullion type

Sovereigns of the 1970s and 1980s are generally traded at their bullion value. They contain 7.32 grammes of fine gold. Particularly perfect examples may be worth a slight premium. The dates struck were as follows:

1974, 1976, 1978, 1979, 1980, 1981 and 1982	Bullion Value

Modern bullion type sovereigns, from 2000 to date, tend to sell for a little more than bullion value as follows (very new coins can sell for more):

	£240.00 to £290.00

Sovereigns, cased proof type

1979		£300.00
1980		£300.00
1981		£300.00
1982		£300.00
1983		£300.00
1984		£300.00
1985		£320.00
1986		£310.00
1987		£310.00
1988		£320.00
1989	500th Anniversary of the Sovereign reverse	£1100.00
1990		£330.00
1991		£330.00
1992		£330.00
1993		£330.00
1994		£330.00
1995		£330.00
1996		£330.00
1997		£330.00
1998		£330.00
1999		£330.00
2000		£330.00
2001		£330.00
2002	Shield reverse	£330.00
2003		£330.00
2004		£330.00
2005 to 2013	(2005 and 2012 had alternate St. George reverses)	£330.00
2014* and 2015		£450.00
2016		£500.00
2017		£600.00

* Also reported with proof reverse and normal BU obverse.

Half Sovereigns, loose bullion type

Until recently, the 1982 Half Sovereign was the only non-proof coin and continues to trade at approximately bullion value. In 2000 the Royal Mint started issuing non-proof half sovereigns and have done so each year since. The 2000 to 2007 half sovereigns tend to trade from about £130 to £160 (based on the bullion value at the time of writing). The 1989 and 2002 shield reverse coins and the St. George 2005 coin are the most popular.

Half Sovereigns, cased proof type

1979		£140.00
1980		£160.00
1981		£150.00
1982		£150.00
1983		£150.00
1984		£150.00
1985		£150.00
1986		£150.00
1987		£150.00
1988		£150.00
1989	500th Anniversary of the Sovereign reverse	£400.00
1990		£150.00
1991		£150.00
1992		£150.00
1993		£150.00
1994		£150.00
1995		£150.00
1996		£150.00
1997		£150.00
1998		£150.00
1999		£150.00
2000		£150.00
2001		£160.00
2002	Shield reverse	£180.00
2003		£160.00
2004		£160.00
2005	Alternate St. George reverse	£180.00
2006		£160.00
2007		£160.00
2008 to 2013	(2012 had alternate St George reverse type)	£160.00
2014 and 2015		£200.00
2016		£250.00
2017		£300.00

Quarter Sovereigns

Introduced in 2009 as a made-up denomination (quarter of a sovereign is a crown, isn't it?) - they seem to sell for £90 - £150, both bullion and proof issue.

152

1980	10,000	£5, £2, Sovereign (£1), 1/2 Sovereign	£3000.00
1981	–	Set containing 9 coins including silver Crown	£1000.00
1982	2,500	£5, £2, Sovereign (£1), 1/2 Sovereign	£3000.00
1983		£2, Sovereign (£1), 1/2 Sovereign	£900.00
1984	7,095	£5, Sovereign (£1), 1/2 Sovereign	£1500.00
1985	5,849	£5, £2, Sovereign (£1), 1/2 Sovereign	£3000.00
1986	12,000	£2 Commonwealth Games, Sovereign (£1), 1/2 Sovereign	£1000.00
1987	12,500	£2, Sovereign (£1), 1/2 Sovereign	£850.00
1988	12,500	£2, Sovereign (£1), 1/2 Sovereign	£950.00
1989	5,000	£5, £2, Sovereign (£1), 1/2 Sovereign (Anniversary reverse)	£3500.00
	7,936	£2, Sovereign (£1), 1/2 Sovereign (Anniversary reverse)	£2000.00
1990	1,721	£5, £2, Sovereign (£1), 1/2 Sovereign	£3100.00
	1,937	£2, Sovereign (£1), 1/2 Sovereign	£1000.00
1991	1,336	£5, £2, Sovereign (£1), 1/2 Sovereign	£3100.00
	1,152	£2, Sovereign (£1), 1/2 Sovereign	£1000.00
1992	1,165	£5, £2, Sovereign (£1), 1/2 Sovereign	£3100.00
	967	£2, Sovereign (£1), 1/2 Sovereign	£1000.00
1993	1,078	£5, £2, Sovereign (£1), 1/2 Sovereign (Pistrucci medallion)	£3300.00
	663	£2, Sovereign (£1), 1/2 Sovereign	£1200.00
1994	918	£5, £2 (Bank of England), Sovereign (£1), 1/2 Sovereign	£3100.00
	1,249	£2 (Bank of England), Sovereign (£1), 1/2 Sovereign	£1100.00
1995	718	£5, £2 (Dove of Peace), Sovereign (£1), 1/2 Sovereign	£3100.00
	1,112	£2 (Dove of Peace), Sovereign (£1), 1/2 Sovereign	£1200.00
1996	742	£5, £2, Sovereign (£1), 1/2 Sovereign	£3100.00
	868	£2, Sovereign (£1), 1/2 Sovereign	£1200.00
1997	860	£5, £2 (bi-metallic), Sovereign (£1), 1/2 Sovereign	£3100.00
	817	£2 (bi-metallic), Sovereign (£1), 1/2 Sovereign	£1200.00
1998	789	£5, £2, Sovereign (£1), 1/2 Sovereign	£3100.00
	560	£2, Sovereign (£1), 1/2 Sovereign	£1100.00
1999	991	£5, £2 (Rugby World Cup), Sovereign (£1), 1/2 Sovereign	£3100.00
	912	£2 (Rugby World Cup), Sovereign (£1), 1/2 Sovereign	£1300.00
2000	1,000	£5, £2, Sovereign (£1), 1/2 Sovereign	£3200.00
	1,250	£2, Sovereign (£1), 1/2 Sovereign	£1200.00

2017 Sovereign - a reproduced version of the original
sovereign reverse (1817 - 1820) was used to mark the
200th anniversary of the sovereign.

2001	1,000	£5, £2 (Marconi), Sovereign (£1), 1/2 Sovereign	£2100.00
	891	£2 (Marconi), Sovereign (£1), 1/2 Sovereign	£1200.00
2002	3,000	£5, £2, Sovereign (£1), 1/2 Sovereign (Shield reverse)	£2400.00
	3,947	£2, Sovereign (£1), 1/2 Sovereign.(Shield reverse)	£1400.00
2003	2,250	£5, £2, Sovereign (£1), 1/2 Sovereign	£2000.00
	1,717	£2 (DNA), Sovereign (£1), 1/2 Sovereign	£1100.00
2004	2,250	£5, £2, Sovereign (£1), 1/2 Sovereign	£2000.00
	2,500	£2, £1 (Forth Bridge), 1/2 Sovereign	£1100.00
2005	1,500	£5, £2, Sovereign (£1), 1/2 Sovereign	£2100.00
	2,500	£2, Sovereign (£1), 1/2 Sovereign	£1100.00
2006	1,750	£5, £2, Sovereign (£1), 1/2 Sovereign	£2000.00
	1,750	£2, Sovereign (£1), 1/2 Sovereign	£1200.00
2007		Sovereign, 1/2 Sovereign	£450.00
	700	£2, Sovereign, 1/2 Sovereign	£1200.00
2008		Sovereign, 1/2 Sovereign	£450.00
		£5, £2, Sovereign, 1/2 Sovereign	£2000.00
		£2, Sovereign, 1/2 Sovereign	£1100.00
2009		£5, £2, Sovereign, 1/2 Sovereign and new 1/4 Sovereign	£2400.00
		£2, Sovereign, 1/2 Sovereign and new 1/4 Sovereign	£1050.00
2010		£5, £2, Sovereign, 1/2 Sovereign, 1/4 Sovereign. Issue price	£2550.00
		Sovereign, 1/2 Sovereign, 1/4 Sovereign. Issue price	£550.00
		'Premium' set, 3 coins as above. Issue price	£1030.00

Values of later sets are similar. They are a lot more expensive when bought new.

Based on a tradition dating back to the 12th century, every year on Maundy Thursday (the day before Good Friday), the monarch distributes leather pouches of special coins to selected people in a Royal Ceremony. The number of recipients is equal to the age of the monarch, as is the value of the coins in each pouch.

All Maundy coinage issued under the reign of Queen Elizabeth II carries the same obverse portrait, that of the first bust of the Queen used on coins and designed by Mary Gillick. On decimalisation day in 1971 the Maundy coins were re-valued from old pence to new pence.

Prices listed here are for complete sets in official Royal Mint cases, which became standard in the 1960s. Commencing in 1989, the coins are individually encapsulated within the case.

1971	1,018	Tewkesbury Abbey	£190.00
1972	1,026	York Minster	£200.00
1973	1,004	Westminster Abbey	£190.00
1974	1,042	Salisbury Cathedral	£190.00
1975	1,050	Peterborough Cathedral	£190.00
1976	1,158	Hereford Cathedral	£190.00
1977	1,138	Westminster Abbey	£190.00
1978	1,178	Carlisle Cathedral	£190.00
1979	1,188	Winchester Cathedral	£190.00
1980	1,198	Worcester Cathedral	£190.00
1981	1,178	Westminster Abbey	£190.00
1982	1,218	St. David's Cathedral, Dyfed	£190.00
1983	1,228	Exeter Cathedral	£190.00
1984	1,238	Southwell Minster	£190.00
1985	1,248	Ripon Cathedral	£200.00
1986	1,378	Chichester Cathedral	£120.00
1987	1,390	Ely Cathedral	£120.00
1988	1,402	Lichfield Cathedral	£190.00
1989	1,353	Birmingham Cathedral	£190.00
1990	1,523	Newcastle Cathedral	£190.00
1991	1,384	Westminster Abbey	£190.00
1992	1,424	Chester Cathedral	£190.00
1993	1,440	Wells Cathedral	£190.00
1994	1,433	Truro Cathedral	£190.00
1995	1,466	Coventry Cathedral	£200.00
1996	1,629	Norwich Cathedral	£200.00
1997	1,786	Bradford Cathedral	£200.00
1998	1,654	Portsmouth Cathedral	£200.00
1999	1,676	Bristol Cathedral	£200.00
2000	1,684	Lincoln Cathedral	£200.00
2000	13,180	silver proof set, taken from special "Millennium Proof Set"	£200.00
2001	1,706	Westminster Abbey	£200.00
2002	1,678	Canterbury Cathedral	£200.00

2002	2,002	gold proof set, taken from special "Golden Jubilee Proof Set".	£1100.00
2003		Gloucester Cathedral	£200.00
2004		Liverpool (Anglican) Cathedral	£200.00
2005		Wakefield Cathedral	£200.00
2006		Guildford Cathedral	£220.00
2007		Manchester Cathedral	
2008		St. Patrick's Cathedral, Armagh	
2009		St. Edmundsbury Cathedral, Suffolk	
2010		Derby Cathedral	
2011		Westminster Abbey	
2012		York Minster	
2013		Christ Church Cathedral, Oxford	
2014		Blackburn Cathedral	
2015		Sheffield Cathedral, South Yorkshire	
2016		St Georges Chapel, Windsor	
2017			

A FEW NOTED ERROR COINS

Error coins have always been very hard to value. It is true for any coin, but is particularly valid for most error coins, that they really are worth what someone is willing to pay for them, as by their very nature they are often unique. Other error types exist in larger numbers (e.g. the 2008 mule 20p, 1983 NEW PENCE 2p etc) and for those the demand for them sets the value. Generally though, most error coins, even quite obscure ones are actually lower value than you may think.

Some errors are mentioned thoughout the book in their appropriate sections. Here are some more that I've noted fairly randomly over the years:

1971 double headed half penny, sold for £200 (20+ years ago)
1971 Penny struck in brass - UNC, sold for £50 in 2014
1980 2p on 22mm flan (smaller) off centre - EF, sold recently for £20
1980 2p in cupro-nickel - AUNC, sold recently for £80
1985 2p in cupro-nickel - VF, sold recently for £300
1983 20p on brass 20mm flan - sold for £50 in 2016
1998 20p on 1p planchet - UNC, sold for £180 in 2016

The Cover Image.

The image on the cover of this book shows the Jody Clark fifth portrait of the Queen, which was introduced in March 2015. In the background are some faint images of recent coin reverses: The 2017 Canute Crown, 2016 Peter Rabbit 50p, 2016 Jemina Puddleduck 50p, 2016 Squirell Nutkin 50p, the 2016 Welsh Dragon £20 coin, 2017 Sir Isaac Newton 50p, 2017 proof Sovereign and the new 12-sided £1 coin.